Leadership Strategy and Tactics Guidebook for Managers

Leadership styles To Lead like a Champ with Charisma Myth & ModernLeaders Strategies and to Win Leadership Challenges inan Organization

Written byBrent T. Donvan

Table of Contents

Chapter 1: Introduction to Leadership

Leadership comes from all over the world. It can be found in all of us. Throughout this book, you will see several examples of leadership. You can learn from those examples. Use the knowledge found in this book to apply to your own style of leadership.

I will talk about different leadership styles. You will learn techniques and skills that will help you move into a higher plain of leadership. We will be guided through the process of creating your own leadership philosophy. Use the information given to elevate your leadership and become the type of leader your team expects you to be, and the type of leader you know you can be.

Being an exceptional leader is not easy to achieve. It takes work and dedication. It takes you to have the willpower to lead, guide, and influence your team. Show them success by being successful. Take the time to examine the great leaders of our past. What made them great? What made them the leader the world sees them as?

"If your actions inspire others to dream more, learn more, do more and become more, you are a leader," as stated by the late former United States president John Quincy Adam. This is an understanding that leadership is pure action-based and preferably not a title or an authority. A leader is only a title anybody can hold buthas an impact that is not everybody's niche. To comprehend, leadership is not about having the authority to rule an organization or perhaps a group of people. Still, the most significant leadership essencehas the influence to inspire others to reach specific goals. It is always about becoming the motivation and creating a group's impact within the industry or within the organization.

The definition and image can be found in different natures and walks of life, from the primary family down to the highest position a person can have, the country's leader. Every group of people who serves a common goal needs a leader to become the driving force of their group; hence, this person's role is critical and essential. It is also the leader's role to convert his power of authority into positive motivation in achieving some desired outcomes.

Different kinds of leaders exist throughout history and today.Depending on the industry and business they represent, they have their own set of criteria for making a leader. These people act based on their subordinates' needs and based on the goals they are set to achieve. For instance, the leader of a church leads his followers base on biblical statements, yet the father, as the head of the family, works to provide peace in the home. Their goals are what determines their actions. Each leader is different,yet they all toil towards their own aspirations and outcomes.

We enumerate the different roles of leadership based on what business they attend to. These leaders usually lead the most common group of people.

Leadership in the Familyis the Driving Force of Exceptional Leadership

The father is considered the *"head of the family."* This is a term commonly used to describe an authority setting within the family lineage. Thisposition is mostly dominated by men; however, certain factors transfer this title to the opposite gender. Leadership creates the necessary decisions that could impact a child's growth and development. In most cases, a child mirrors his parents' actions, making the parent's gesture condemnatory. The head of the family needs to become a positive influencer to other members of his line by being aware of his actions by making the right decisions, and creating a safe and sound atmosphere. Historically, the father is written in biblical structure to be tasked to labor and toilfor them to provide for his family's needs.

The responsibility of a father does not only limit his capacity to provide for his family's needs. The head of a home is not just a title but rather a function.There are plenty of leadership roles for him to fit in, such as staying faithful to his wife, involving his wife in all decisions he makes, protecting his home against outside discrepancies, disciplining the children, and many others.

To provide leadership to a family is through serving the needs of the family. Ruling over their loved ones is not just about giving orders but rather about showing empathy and helping with things, no matter if they are big or small. After all, fathers should model their children the proper way to behave and how to treat others. Effective leadership at home maintains a feeling of peace. Thus, the head of a family is critical to bring peace in their home.

In the times of old, leadership in the family was viewed differently. Today, it takes both parents to raise children. Each parent has their own role to play that brings leaders together as one. You can compare the family unit to an organization or business. There is a magician in Las Vegas who performs at a casino every night. His whole crew is his family. Each member of his family has a different role to play. He is the performer. His wife takes care of the showgirls in turns on who goes on stage, what they wear, and their hair. His father helps build the equipment that goes on stage with the magician for the magic to work. Finally, his mother is in control of the lighting. In this family show, each member plays their part. The same is in the leadership of the family.

In my family, we each have a vital role to play. Granted, my wife does more than me, and I am very grateful for what she does. I work to support our family financially so that we will always have money to survive. My wife cleans the house, cooks, homeschools our daughter, takes care of the budget, and so on. She tells me when to pay bills, and I take care of them. When it comes to family trips or big decisions, we work together. It is essential to always have leadership as a team to raise a family. A great parent can raise a child, but exceptional parents can raise a leader.

A Great Parent Can Raise a Child, but Exceptional Parents can
Raise a Leader.

This leadership as a couple is becoming less and less. It can be a struggle to find parents who have these leadership qualities. I oftensee parents who would rather be friends to their child instead of putting their foot down to discipline them because it will make them mad or upset.

Keep in mind, there is a way of disciplining your children and still show your love. That is what an exceptional leader does. It does not matter who is the *"head"* of your family. It could be the husband or the wife. However, the real "head" of every family is the parents. You must work together as a team. How do you be a leader in your own family? The answer is as easy as 1... 2... 3....

The best part, these same leadership qualities pass over into the role of a manager or leader in an organization. You should treat your team as your family. In an organization, you have a board of directors that help managers to run the business. While in the family, your board of directors is the family unit. It takes a team to run a team. You expect your family to follow the rules and behaviors within the family unit. In business, you also have a type of behavior that must be adhered to in the workplace.

You do not raise them from birth as a child. However, you do introduce them within your team and watch them grow to become a leader. As a father, you want your children to have a better life than you, while you want your team to become a better leader than yourself. You show them how to be a leader.

You expect your children to explore and allow them to learn on their own. They will make mistakes. Within your team, they will also make mistakes. As a leader, you will be there to pick them up and help them through their journey. You will do the same with your team. You are their guide to show them how to work through it.

Set the example and expect respect: This may be straight forward to most of us. In fact, you are probably looking at me and see, *"well, that is a no brainer."* In the military, I learned that common sense rules are put in writing because someone does not have the common sense to do the right thing.

The real question is, *"how do you expect respect from your children or team if you do not show them respect?"* I want you to think about it. How would you answer this simple question? The truth is, you cannot expect respect if you do not give the same consideration. It is the same with any situation you ever face as a leader.

You are the example for your children or your team. If they do not seeyou respect them or others, they will not know how to respect them. This goes with any leadership position you may have.

Do not justify yourself: So many parents feel they need to explain the decisions. You do not need too. They are your children, and they should trust your choices are for a reason. They should be confident in what you decide. You cannot expect your children to be optimistic if you are not. I hear this a lot, *"the parent's response is: I was once your age and have done it all."* Most parents have not done it all. However, they are confident when they tell it to their children.

Being a family leader does not mean you will please your children in every decision you make. There are times they may hate you. In the end, they will also thank you for the decision you made.

The same goes for being a leader. As a leader, you must be confident. Even if you are not sure of the answer, you must show that you know. Your team must see that you are behind whatever decision you make. If you second guess yourself, your team will do the same with you as a leader.

Communication is essential: As a leader, you want to teach how to communicate effectively. This does not mean using bad wordsfound in the dictionary. If someone did that to me, I would turn my back on them and stop listening. That is never an effective way to communicate.

I am talking about showing your children how to express themselves. Show them how to vent about what positively is on their minds. It is the same in the business. You are there to listen to your team. You must know what is going on outside organizations.If they are not taught this, they will be the first example and think using all kinds of foul language is the right way. If your team does not trust you as a leader, they will not be willing to talk to you. This involved effectively listening to your team members. If they feel you do not hear or communicate with them, they will thinkthat working with you is boring and will not advance their careers.

Communication is essential for you to achieve your goals. This is the same for any form of environment. It will create a good relationship between you and your team;instead, your family or any organization you are with. Effective communication brings interaction and draws you closer together. It will help the productivity of your team as you are continuously sharing information as you receive it. As data is given to everyone, it sets the standards to fully understand the tasks, terms, conditions, and requirements.

Stand behind your decisions: This is one of the hardest parts of being a family leader. There will be times you have to tell your children something they do not like. They may even hate you for some time. Even within your team, you may need to decide they will not agree on. Your team members may even hate you or your decision. This is where good communication takes part in leadership. You let them know the reason behind the decision that was made. Your team may not fully understand why you made that decision when there may be a better way of doing things. When you stand firm, it means your team members must know that the decision is not negotiable. It is the same with your children.

Depending on the situation, you may want your children to have a chance to tell you how they are feeling. Letting your children or team share their feelings will open the communication line, and you will understand where the problems came from and how to solve them. For example, in a business, you need ideas and information to help you find the issues and fix them. If you do not know the problems, you cannot develop a game plan for those issues. This is also part of leadership.

Being a leader in a family will be the most challenging leadership role you will have. It will be a challenge. You will make decisions that affect your family. However, it will also prepare you to become a leader in the workplace.

I found many of the best leaders are parents. They treat their team as a family. If there is a better way of doing things, ask your team. However, there are times that it must be done a specific way to complete the task. That is when you explain your choices and how it needs to be done to avoid conflict.

Do not Have Favoritism: Many parents play favoritism in the family. They may like one child more than another, which forces resentment among your children. This could be due to various reasons. Perhaps you like one more due to the are more like you than the other. Regardless of the reason, harmony in the family is broken. It is the same with your team or organization.

When the manager or leader shows favoritism, resentment among your team members form. They feel you like one member better than themself. They become jealous of the other person. This will lower productivity in the team as they are always trying to compete. They want the attention of the boss.

You want to elevate all your team, increase productivity, and understand that each team member has a job. There is not one person who is better than any other person. What one person can do does not mean everyone can do the same job. They are specially trained to do that job.

Leadership in the Workplace

To become a leader in a workplace does not necessarily require a title;moreover, to become a leader is having the influence on his workmates to do more and become better in their job. It is creating the motivation of his workmates to finish any task at hand.

Managers or any person who holds a higher leadership position know leading means to delegating tasks and overseeing their subordinates' operations. As a part of their responsibilities, they must develop skills and learn to become more effective leaders that can positively impact their business, no matter how big or small. The Former First Lady of the United States, Roselyn Carter, said, *"A leader takes people where they want to go. A great leader takes people where they do not necessarily want to go but ought to be."*Managers and people with a higher position in every industry serve as the path walk and direction of their business. It is about them creating the supervision that will lead their subordinates into success.

> *A Leader Takes People where they Want to Go. A Great Leader Takes People where they Do Not Necessarily Want to Do, but Ought to Be.*

A leader's role in a workplace is to engage with his people, influence their way of work, become a part of their business decisions, create a positive workforce environment, and encourage them to act around a common goal. It is making the impression to his subordinates what the company can offer in the long term, which influences the employees' confidence in their work and the company.

These matters may require a bit of work for leaders to learn. There are instances that many leaders in their workforce either lack the skills of leading. They may not understand how to use their skills to guide and give direction to the team. These unfortunate situations deliver a negative result that reflects on their business.

As the most famous saying goes,*"Leaders are not born, but rather made,"* explains that specific skills can be acquired and learned,which will create a compellingand exceptional leader.

I will not be expanding too much in this area, as we will be touching it throughout the book's entirety.

Leaders of the Communityand the Managers Role

A *"community"* represents a group of people with the same interest, purpose and practice. The term community is one of the foundations of modern society (Putnam, 2001). Their goal is to uphold the well-being and interest of its community members. They are mostly non-profit organizations and receive members as volunteers. They are service-oriented who are mostly dedicating themselves to the well-being and lively interest of other people within and outside their group. They aim to create a change by creating a sustainable environment, seeking empowerment, influencing others through peaceful manners, and supplying provisions to peoplein need. The community members work together to create a pleasant place to live,ranging from their own neighborhood to greater distances.

A dedicated and influential community leader knows how to communicate the group's goals to the team. They know how to influence each team member and motivates them to achieve a positive outcome. Desired results depend heavily on the improvement they created, whether in an individual or in a group of people.

Agreat example of community-based organizationsisa parent-teacher organization, charities, book clubs, recycling program community, food drive organization, and so many more.

For example, where I live, the food bank has been given food boxes to help those in need. This is due to a hardship that has hit the world. The food bank allows millions of people who are in dire need every year due to them hitting a rough patch in their lives. This is only one story and a great example of a community-based organization.

Even in these non-profit organizations, they require the leadership of managers. They need someone who takes charge and makes things happen. This is an excellent way to work on your leadership skills. Many companies encourage their members to volunteer. The reason is how the members will have to opportunity to develop their leadership while helping the community. They learn a strong sense of service.

Leaders of the Church are Like Managers of an Organization

The leaders of churches are the stewards of goodwill and teachers of God's word.They oversee the works of mankind and are responsible for maintaining a balance between wrongdoings and humane conduct.

The leadership of thesechurches lies within the boundaries of its members. They are responsible for the Christian growth of their members and the administration of the entirechurch. The leaders are chosen and given the task to work diligently with their members into doing good, take charge of the church, administrate the needs of its members, and the church's elders. They also have the desire to seek out new members.

A church leader has several responsibilities that are associated with leading the church and guiding its members. It may be the same as a manager for a business or company. Theyalso have stewardship of the company and the team. You are responsible for the actions of your team. If you are a leader within the company, you may only have stewardship over a small group. However, if you are the manager, you may have stewardship over several leaders and teams. It is your job to help your team grow and advance in their career. It is the same as a church leader who can help their church grow and prosper in their spirituality.

Government Leadersand their Role for Managers

There is recently an argument between the management style and the challenges of the public and private sectors. Many would agree that the difficulties of running a government are similar to that of a private company. What remains constant is how both sectors need a leader to represent their business to the people.

Being a leader comes with its own challenges. The position requires making the issues the primary purpose of every plan is to resolve the problems before they arise. They must give their team priority over everything else.Servant leadership requires a selfless leader as an essential part of running an office, for the leader's task is creating a more significant impact and change. His success will always be determined by his actions and the differences he makes. Making the position more demanding, complicated, and heavy to anyoneto carrythe title of leader.

Power and authority are combinations of factors associated with a government position. These attributes will bring specific effects that can harm and endanger the life of a leader. It has been proven before that power can destroy a current state of a leader's leadership. Too much use can lead to harmful effects such as losing a career, imprisonment, personal relationships ruined or losing one's state of mind.

A government leader must always be handlingthe power and authority that is given to them carefully. It should be managed carefully for worthwhile cause only and should not be mismanaged to avoid harm.

You can learn a lot from a leader in the government. Many of the same qualities are needed in running both the government and your team. You should run your team like congress runs the United States. Look at how congress is organized. Learn from it. They each have a role to play. It takes a vote to pass a bill. They work together. It takes a nation to vote for a new president that will take charge of the country. The same goes forleading your team. It takes your team to make effective decisions and increase productivity.

These are only some of the many examples of businesses, industries, and sectors wherein leadershipis essential. Yet, there has always been someone who is the team leader in every industry or group of people.A leader plays a vital role in an almost senseless part of every leader in the world.

Throughout the book, I will talk about several definitions of leadership, different leadership types, the qualities and characteristics of a leader, what ways you can become a significant or exceptional leader, and the different leadership styles. The aims areto promote the importance of leadership and its differences if it could be handledin a right or wrong way.

You will tackle different strategies for making yourself acquainted with becoming an effective and efficient leader. You will be able to materialize the proper way of leading a team and successfully reaching your goals. However, one must remember to maintain patience and continue working with perseverance for becoming an effective leader or leaders in this long road of exceptional leadership. Overall, this is a learning processyou will learn as you go, and the results of your work depend on the amount of determination and perseverance you put into your leadership. Buckle up and let us take this exciting adventure together.

Chapter 2: The Workings of Leadership

There are no actual words that can describe the fundamental attributes, for the definition of leadership has various meanings, images, and examples. To summarize it all, leadership is not all about a person's personality traits but is described through the actions and changes it creates.

Some facts can generally define the meaning of leadership. Here are some of the fantasticattributes of leadership:

Leaders are influencers: This is the strength of a leader that can be determined with their capacity to influence people. They impact their motivation, becoming an inspiration and a beacon of hope are the major determining factors of their influence.

Great Learners: They acknowledge the fact that leadership is a learning process. They accept the reality that their leadership quality is determined by the length of time they have been in a leadership position.Great leaders give importance to self-development and continuous learning.

Voracious readers: In connection to the continuous learning process of being a leader, a great leader will derive from being a voracious reader.An abundance of excellent leaders in history is known to be diligent readers. There are several success stories about leading that can be found in books.

Agents of change: Leaders areallowed to lead people tobecome a catalyst of change. They promote growth in the lives of their people, focusing on turning their vision into reality. Great leaders create an impact on the lives of many and encourage inspiration through leading by example.

Leaders inspire and motivate: Leading by example is dictated by the actions and behaviors a leader shows their team. A great leader knows how to inspire and motivate people. Here are some consistent behaviors a leader portrays through influencing and motivation:

> * They have a clear vision of the future state of their team and what they want to accomplish.
> * They create a strong connection with their team by extending help and physical presence when necessary.
> * They deliver philosophy to let their team know what is expected of them.
> * They walk the talk by delivering their promises through their actions.
> * They are enthusiastic and displays positivism in all the things they handle, through their actions, and the words they say.
> * They make use of their experience as a tool to sharpen their leadership skills.

> They are competent in what they do, and they never stop the learning process.

The Art of Performing

Leaders that are competent while show as consistent in performing and delivering positive results. They use the best of their abilities and resources are given to them. They never stop learning, growing, and improving as they are determined to become better in each given opportunity.

They remain consistent in being an effective leader in this ever-changing world.Here are some of the best examples where leaders perform at their best.

Personal Growth: Leaders acknowledge the need for self-development and growth. They foresee the benefits aspects leadership can provide rather than focusing on the challenges. They know that continuous development is the determinant of success for being a great leader that others will want to follow.

They invested and took the risk of becoming a better person by working with a mentor, attending workshops, enrolling in training, and aiming for experiences to develop their qualities and characteristics.

Performers must be self-starters: The best leadership starts within you, your values,and your morals. A leader must be motivated and practice initiative in handling essential things. They must be less supervised in dealing with complicated matters, yet they must perform accordingly. A great leader starts with having a great attitude with a great purpose that starts within themselves.

Lead the change: Leaders create the change they want to see, which usually starts within themselves. They become better leaders by instilling change in themselves through physical or personal traits. They build their reputation based on what they contribute to the lives of their people.

Creates a positive work culture: A positive culture is composed of people who are enthusiastic about being a part of the team, who maintains a pleasant attitude in handling challenges, and remains optimistic about performing.

Embody a positive attitude: As a self-starter, a great leader creates the change they wanted others to see through their own actions and appearance.They become a significant influencer and motivator by showing self-gratitude; hence this positivism will radiate among their members, which is beneficial for the team.The only thing that makes it better is by reflecting this positivism consistently throughout their leadership.Here are some ways on how a leader can embody a positive attitude:

- Share your smile with the people you encounter. This shows your kindness.
- Start journalizing the positive things that happen to you daily.
- Create a positive habit and an optimistic mindset.

The Art of Leading with Exceptional Leadership

Every style of leadership varies from situation to situation while combining the attitudes of people. A leader relies on a variety of circumstances and the people they are dealing with. They create their strategies based on the challenge they face and the level of difficulty each challenge produces.

Leadership is the art of leading. However, not all people have the capacity to lead people, or not all people have the *"leadership calling,"* so as they say. The ability to manage, control and make difficult decisions are more challenging than any given task. It takes years to practice becoming an efficient leader and experience of being in chargeof being called an exceptional leader.

Abusive Leadership

Often, the workforce leaders are under too much stress that they break down in front of their employees. Being an abusive leader comes in many forms, whether it is a boss lashing out at his employees, being lazy, or bullying himself and creating self-doubts. The bad bosses' phenomenon is making employees leave their jobs, turn companies into having profit losses, and create an unhealthy work environment. Typically, what causes bad bosses are the circumstances they lose control of.

An abusive leader's definition is based on certain factors such as their subordinates' perception of their leadership style, which is composed of their behaviors, responses,the way they criticize or is determined by their hostility. It can also be manifested through the way they give orders, which they engage in abusive supervision.

Abusive leadership is a cycle that affects every individual concern negatively, either physically or psychologically. The process usually starts with the leader criticizing his employee for being incompetent, then the employee develops fear, which then triggers other behavior such as avoidance or skipping work. It then causes attitudes that affect the company's performance, which the upper management will reprimand the so-called boss of the employee who is repeatedly repeating the same cycle.

The consequences of having a lousy boss generally goes both ways, with bullying on both sides. The employees develop anxieties and self-doubts while the boss tends to have more conflicts at home and work. Either way, both people experience an unfortunate consequence.

As an argument, many people will agree that an abusive leader exists in almost every workplace. Ifadverse effects attribute to every challengeof being a leader, abusive leadership will prevail. The following are the characteristics and traits of abusive supervision.

He uses his power and authority to receive personal favors from people: Nothing worse than a corrupt leader. Often, people with authority and power are associated with illicit actions detrimental to their position and the business they represent. Abusive leaders use bribes to extract personal favors and use their power to pave their way out in facing the consequences.

They threaten and manipulate people to get what they want: They use their position to create an image of being better than the people they lead. They resort to ways such as political, monetary, or psychological leverage to make them obey. They manipulate them into doing things beyond their job description by offering fear of losing their job or something valuable to them.

Serving people is the least of their concern: They become leadersas they are attracted to the position's power and authority. Serving and leading is the least of their situation;instead, they focus too muchon what their work can provide. They often leave their responsibility to other people without having to acknowledge their sacrifices.

They prey on weak minds: An abusive leader preys on the weakest link as they are easy to manipulate. These individuals are most likely to be in power; hence they become more vulnerable and naïve. They keep their distance from smart, confident, and independent people as they will be exposedto their adverse actions.

They control the weak be feeding them off and isolating them: After leading the weak, they separate them and leave them farther from the group to continue to manage them. This is also to take advantage of their vulnerability, making them more dependent on their leader's attention given to them.They often make them fragile by taking care of their needs, monetarily and emotionally, thus making them more dependent.

They demand absolute loyalty: In connection with taking control, abusive leaders do not favor their people to receive help from others. They requirecomplete control from them by making them feel guilty about the things they receive from the leader.

Leaders who use this method feel threatened when their subordinates search for aid or become less dependent on them.

They use the blackmail method to eliminate conscience: Abusive leaders who do not get what they want to usea blackmail method to threaten the person they want something from. They use monetary value, personal relationships, family members, and other valuable things they can use against them for their favor.

They use others for their own personal agenda: Self-satisfaction was always the goal of these leaders. They become the person with power and authority, so then they will comprehend the feeling of superiority. Naturally, they exchange their people's sacrifices for self-gratification.

They quickly get angry when things do not go as they want: Exhibiting rage and anger when the deserved results are not achieved, or things will not go in their way.They tend to blame people for producing incompetent results rather than taking responsibility for their own actions. They do not practice self-control when they are in rage and feeling angry. They display their violent emotions to make people understand that they demand more of their efforts and sacrifices.

They are narcissists: They are motivated by their need for power and self-gratification rather thantheir team's concern. They use their leadership as a platform to satisfy their ego and elevate their lifestyle. They are only interested in pleasing themselves even if it means sacrificing the detriment of others.

The things listed above are the qualities of an abusive leader. Abusive leader behaviors involve dominance, being arrogance, selfishness, and hostile tendencies towards other people. They are driven by their own personal need to lead rather than serve the real cause of being a leader. I will discuss this in a later chapter as we focus on not becoming an abusive leader.

Chapter 3: The Substance of Leadership

Leadership is known all over the world. It is an essential part of a business and any organization. Imagine a world without direction. What would that world be like? I imagine you see disorganization and chaos. You will see businesses closing their doors and failing. You would know the school systems failing and children without education. The list goes on and on.

Hold onto that picture as you go through this chapter. While you are reading, start to add the things I talk about in your mind. Start picturing your world-changing as you introduce leadership. By the time you finish this chapter, you will see and understand the importance of leadership.

Having a Clear Vision

When you start a business, organize an event, or do anything as a group that requires working together, it is essential to have a clear vision. I had seen times when there were too many people trying to be the boss or leader andcould not work together. There was chaos.

There should be one person who has a clear vision and understanding of the task. That person starts to bring the organization into the group. The best example of this is through the military. In the military, there is a commander. The commander relays information to the first sergeant. It then goes to a detachment sergeant, squad leader, and finally to the soldiers. This type of leadership ensures data is delivered to everyone within the organization. If the military did not have this type of leadership, there would be missed information, and no one will have a clear picture of what is needed.

Having a leader who has this vision will bring strength and guidance to the group. You will start to see the organization forming. Take the time to go make to your world of no leadership and add people who have a clear vision. This alone will start to change the way your world looks.

Planning Effectively

This is great. You now have leaders in your world who have clear visions or pictures of what is needed for the organizations. Knowing what needs to be done is one thing; however, do they know how to accomplish it?

Effective leadership requires planning. You cannot have oversightwithout knowing how to plan. Imagine going into a meeting, and the presenter did not intend for it? How would that meeting turnout?Imagine going to class, and your teacher did not prepare the lesson for that day. Will you learn anything or want to listen to the teacher?

It is essential to have a plan. Without a plan, you will not have direction, and there will continue to be chaos.Look at your world with leaders and add each of your leaders to be useful planners.

Inspire and Motivate

This is great. You have a world with leaders who are useful planners. However, what are the people like? Are they happy? The only leadership they see are those who can plan. Yet, they give jobs that are not pleasing to the people, and the leaders do not care.

Not every task a leader has is pleasant. It is vital to inspire and motivate others to do the right thing. Give them a reason to do the job. Sometimes, telling them how much they are appreciated will go a long way in leadership.

Look at your world and include inspiration and motivation in your leaders. How has your world changed? You now have leadership that involves effective planning, motivation, and inspiration.

Willingness to Try New Ideas

You have created some outstanding leadership in your world. Your leaders are useful planners who can motivate and inspire others. It is time to see advancement.

You can have an effective organization if all you do is inspire, motivate, and plan. Although you will not move forward. You will not see advancement in your world if you are unwilling to try new ideas and things.

During my time in the military, as a leader, I was always given tasks that I did not like, and I must obey the orders and guidance given to me. My leadership would still want me to do it their way. I looked at the task, and no matter what I did to motivate my soldiers, they were not happy and were always complaining.I started to look at it from a different perspective and began trying new ideas to finish the task. I showed the outcome of my leadership, and they were pleased. It helped the organization move forward instead of staying in the same old loop of doing things.

Add trying new things to your leadership in your world. You should start seeing progression. Your world will no longer sit still. Do you think Henry Ford would succeed with the Ford Automotive Company if he were unwilling to try new things? A successful organization or business will only see advancement if they are willing to think outside of the box.

Relationships with the Members of the Group

I am not talking about taking members of your organization on a date. However, I am talking about knowing everyone under your leadership. This includes knowing them, their needs, and their families. You accomplish this by working side-by-side with them. The goal is to have employees or group members feel comfortable about coming to you about anything. They work hard for you; you should work hard for them. Add the relationship between the leadership and those they lead to your mental world.

Integrity is Essential

A key aspect of leadership has integrity. It is a leader's job to always be honest with their dealings. It is also the leader's job to pass this same element along to those they are over. Being open and having integrity will help a business to excel. The last thing you want is leadership that turns there back when something is wrong and pretend it did not happen.

For example, a business has several leaders. Most of them have integrity and do the right thing. However, a leader is working the bookkeeping for the company and records a transaction for a trip to Hawaii but listed it as a business trip to its headquarters. The leader got a free trip to Hawaii at the expense of the business. This also costs the business money. If this happens often, it could also put the companyinto financial trouble.

So far, you have a pretty good world forming in your mind. Add integrity to your leadership.

Ability to Act in a Crisis

Every organization will face adversity. There will be challenges and possibly emergencies the organization will face. A leader needs to know how to react in these situations. They need to *"think on their feet."*

Let us take it a step further. A leader needs to train everyone in the organization to let them know what they should do in each situation. This is not an easy thing to do. You cannot plan for every unexpected situation. Yet, a leader must act fast and handle it.

Finally, take all these aspects of leadership and add the ability to act in a crisis. How did your world turn out? You can see how these simple things can transform a world of chaos into a world of order and organization. The world needs leadership to survive. Without supervision, the world would be disast ous.

Chapter 4: Leadership Theories

Leadership has been around for decades. In the past, people always thought leaders were born with the ability to lead. They called them *"born leaders."* That way of thinking kept a lot of good leaders hidden. They would think, *"their parents are leaders, so they are born leaders."* With that thought in mind, it made others who do not have leaders in the family think they could never be a leader. What do you think? Do you need to be born into leadership, or can it be developed?

For centuries, researchers have been trying to find the perfect formula for exceptional leadership. Look at the leaders around us. It does not matter if they are your direct leader or the President of the United States. You have seen evil, right, and exceptional leadership in all the roles. Yet, we still wonder about leadership. I have seen Presidents who I would not think would be a good leader and turned out to be very good at running the country. Yet, I have seen the opposite where a very successful business becomes president and is horrible in the president's role. The truth is, born leaders are not good leaders in every situation. Leaders' ability to lead must be developed. Thus, was born **The Great Man Theories**.

Several other theories could be considered with leadership.

Trait Theories

These theories focus on a specific variable that will relate to the environment. They may be determined by a particular style of leadership that will be best for each situation. Based on the trait theory, no one type of leadership works for every situation. It is not only about your leadership qualities. It is more about hitting the exact science betweenneeds, context, and behaviors.

Situational Theories

These theories are based on the best course of action, depending on the situation. Leaders are faced with hard decisions every day. The different leadership styles will determine the type of move you take for each case. Some techniques are better than other kinds.

Behavioral Theories

These theories are the opposite of the Great Man Theories. These are based on leaders being made; they are not born. Leaders have traits that steam from their personal beliefs. These beliefs make them who they are. Observe the different leaders in history. The most outstanding leaders were not born leaders. They were made leaders from experiences they had in life. These are the type of leaders who are always learning and improving themselves.

Participative Theories

These leaders encourage input from their team. They want everyone to be involved in the decisions that are made. It is always important to allow your team to give feedback and have a say. They will respect the leader more if they know they are heard.

Management Theories

You will typically see management theories in businesses. They thrive on a reward and punishment setting. With the focus placed on organization, group performance, and supervision. Sometimes, it is called transactional theories.

Relationship Theories

These theories bring new light to leadership and can be called transformational ideas. There focus is between the leader and the team. They now the power of inspiration and motivation. They become focused on doing things as a team and have great respect for everyone in the group. However, they also have the highest standards. Yet, they earned the respect of their team, and the criteria are always met or exceeded.

Each of these theories pinpoints that each leader must fit into one of them. Considering that we each have our own personalities and are individuals, most of us will fit into several categories. I have never seen a leader that was a born leader or a leader that was made have only one of these qualities.

Chapter 5: The Fundamentals of a Leadership Psychology

Winston Churchill was a great leader who once said, *"The price of greatness is responsibility."* During the time of Churchill, this is how great leaders were perceived. It would be great if that were all it took to be an exceptional leader. Give me all the responsibility you can. I may be fatigued from all the blame, but I am a great leader. I wish it were that simple. Churchill had a point that leadership does bring more responsibility. However, it is not what makes a leader of any sort.

Psychology shows that there is more to it than having responsibilities. It is not about making a list and checking off tasks as they are completed. Have you ever heard anybody say you are a great leader based on your responsibilities if you are a leader? If that is how others see you as a leader, it is time to reflect on your leadership and figure out what needs to change. Psychology tells us there are some aspects of leadership that Churchill did not know about.

Summoning Your Willpower

For some people, it can be a challenge to summon your willpower. A new leader may also find this difficult. However, the more experienced you are as a leader, the easier it will be. Eventually, this will become second nature. It will be as natural as tying your own shoes.

A leader must have the ability to do many tasks without supervision. It is the leader's job to get them done. Many times, these tasks are not fun or enjoyable. It requires the willpower to do them. The position a leader holds gives them a natural reaction to perform and have self-regulation of their actions.

Through research, they have found that when a person is placed in a leadership role, they will shine as a leader and start making decisions. Does this make them a leader? Yes, if they are guiding a team. Everyone has the potential to be a leader. They start to have a leader's mindset and will have the willpower to learn to become a better leader.

Influential Leadership

Leaders know how to influence others through their actions and by the way they talk. They know how to talk to other leaders and to their team. They positively influence others, regardless of what their competence is. This influence will help them elevate into the social hierarchies. You will find that their forces will make them stick out as a leader in a group setting.

Through their influence, they can inspire and motivate their team. This allows for outstanding performance with the team and the leader.

Motivation and Inspiration from Within

Leaders have a natural way to motivate and inspire their team. Some are born with this, while others have learned to develop this powerful skill. Knowing how to motivate your team is essential for productivity. Knowing how to inspire their team will bring creativity and respect among everyone. This works together with being influential.

Narcissist May Arise in Leaders

This may be something unfamiliar to you. This is when the leader will view themselves essentially and requires admiration from others. These are the type of leaders you insist on taking over the group and being the leader. They want to be the center of attention. The issue with this is their work performance. They are so focused on looking good in front of others that they do not notice their poor work performance. However, even though their own accountfails, they are great at relaying information to the team. They want the team to see him as a great leader. Therefore, making the team have good performance.

Desire to Please Superiors

I have seen it all the time where a leader has the desire to please their superiors. This is one of the most significant issues I found in the United States Military. The Military has a strict hierarchy that must be followed. The lowest leader tries so hard to please his own leaders. This makes it impossible for them to shine as an exceptional leader. The reason is that they are forced to do things in a way that is not their own. They must perform in the way their superiors want them to perform. This is the beginning of their failure. It is the beginning of the collapse of the leader and the inability of the managers.

Keep in mind, many leaders have the willpower and determination to fight the odds. They go above and beyond by doing things their way and showing their superiors what they can do as a leader. This is how they become a better leader. Although, there are cases where this hierarchy works, such as in the Military. The military is such a vast organization, they need order. This hierarchy brings this order. It is the leadership within the scale that tries to please their superiors.

It has become evident that leadership is not straight forward as Churchill has. There is more to it than having responsibilities. This is only the beginning of your understanding of the psychology behind leadership. To indeed be useful and an exceptional leader, you must develop your own sense of psychology. Take the parts you believe in and make them your own. Add them to your way of leadership. It is always a learning process. Focus on the type of leader you want to be and make it happen. Be the leader you know you can be.

Chapter 6: Bad, Good & Exceptional Leadership

Leadership comes in many forms. There is terrible leadership, good leadership, and exceptional leadership. Sometimes, leaders do not realize they are a lousy leader or a good leader. In the eyes of every leader, they see themselves as an exceptional leader. Most leaders fall under bad or good leadership. Very few would be considered excellent.

Leaders are faced with tough decisions every day. Their patience is tested to the limit. Their skills as a leader are challenged. Their mindset is questioned. The lay a leader responds to the different situations will say a lot about their leadership.

It is essential to understand the difference in each situation. I have divided this chapter into three subheadings. Each area will have the same problem. However, the response based on each leadership style will be demonstrated based on a bad leader, a good leader, or an exceptional leader. As you read through the situations, I want you to think about what your response would be.

Bad Leadership

Situation One: You have an employee who approaches you with the idea that could help the team.As a leader, you probably should have already done this, but you have not gotten to it.Think about how you would answer this situation. What would you do?

A bad leader would feel annoyed about everything that is brought to them. They would think that theiremployee is trying to tell them how to be a leader. The leader will do one of three things. They may ignore it entirely and pretend their employee never talked to them. The leader may think of excuses for not acting on the idea. Finally, the leader may think of a way to criticize the employee. How do you think that employee will feel? What do you think they will say about the leader?

In this situation, and with this type of leadership, the employees will never make another suggestion. They will feel it is not worth their effort or time. They will feel low self-esteem. The employees are the front line and will usually have the best ideas to improve the business, yet their ideas will be unheard and dormant. They will complain and talk about the leader behind their back.

Situation Two: Let us shift our focus to another problem. You are in a meeting that is already very long when an employee asks a hard question. The employee questions the values of the project which are being focused on. The employee askes, *"How did you get to this solution?"* They continue with another question by asking, *"What made all of us decide to do it this way in the first place?"*

A bad leader would look at these questions and be offended. They would be shocked because an employee is questioning their leadership. They are thinking, *"how dare them to question me and my decision."* All the leader does is stare at them with an evil eye, turning the subject back to the original discussion.

The effects of the reactions of the leader send ice-cold chills throughout the team. The team knows not to ask challenging and vital questions during the meetings. They go with the flow of things. Having a healthy debate within your team and discussing the issues is like a foreign language.

Situation Three:I want to shift gears a little and focus on having someone on the team that does a job the leader is not familiar with. The leader does not know what is involved in the position; therefore, they do not know what the keys to success are with the job.

As a bad leader, you feel threatened by the new hire. They know somethingthe leader does not know. They are scared that the team will look at them as not knowing everything about everybody's jobs. They have what is called imposter syndrome. That means they fake it and pretend they know what the team member is doing. The leader stays entirely away from the employee and acts like they already know everything about the job.

Based on this bad leadership, the communication between the leader and this team member breaks down quickly. The employee will roll their eyes at the leader's pretentious act when they try to convince them they know what they are talking about. Contention becomes evidentas the employee is pushing the leader to move so they can do their job.

Situation Four:A company thinks the leadership needs a little help. They bring in a coach to help the leaders to improve their leadership. The coach informs a leader they must do something. The leader should have done it before now.

A bad leader will pretend they did not hear the advice from the coach. They will think it is more work. They tell themselves it can wait until later because it does not need to be done for another month. The leader continues to find excuses as to why it is at the bottom of the list of all the other things they need to do. The task does not apply to the leader.

As a result of the leader's thoughts, they miss out on its effects on the team if it is done right away. The coach does not want to guide the leader as they will not listen.

With all these situations, the choices of a bad leader could cause chaos within the team. Eventually, it could cause a demotion of the leader, or they could lose their job completely.

Good Leadership

Situation One: You have an employee who approaches you with the idea that could help the team. As a leader, you probably should have already done this, but you have not gotten to it.

A good leader accepts and embraces the truth. Sometimes it is hard to hear but the leader understands and listens to the employee. The employees see a need and feel comfortable bringing it to the leader because they know they will appreciate and listen to them. The leader will gladly give their feedback on the idea and may even ask questions to better understand.

The result of this type of leadership will allow the employees to feel they have been heard. They will see that your leader makes them a priority. Giving and getting feedback from your team is good team management.

Situation Two: You are in a meeting that is already very long when an employee asks a hard question. The employee questions the values of the project which are being focused on. The employee askes, *"How did you get to this solution?"* They continue with another question by asking, *"What made all of us decide to do it this way in the first place?"*

A good leader will address the questions directly. They will not beat around the bush and give a roundabout answer. Based on the situation, the leader will explain why the decision is made this way. They well let the team know how it will benefit them. The leader may help them better understand the decisions through questions to find the answers themselves. If the problem was disruptive, the leader could later talk to the individualabout that issue and 1 on 1.

They the actions of the leader, the team will see there is no such thing as a dumb question. The unit trusts the leader more and knows it is ok to challenge the leader's decisions. This will also help the team explore ideas that could help everyone.

Situation Three: The company hires someone on the team that does a job the leader is not familiar with. The leader does not know what is involved in the position. They do not know what the keys to success are with the job.

As a good leader, you understand and recognize the lack of knowledge you have with the job. The leader will communicate with the employee and find out what they need. Together they create a plan that the new employee can be accountable for. The leader asks questions and focuses on understanding the position better.

This leader started to build trust with the employee and their team. Even when the leader is not familiar with the job, they tried to understand it created a plan to knowthe expectations.

Situation Four: A company thinks the leadership needs a little help. They bring in a coach to help the leaders to improve their leadership. The coach informs a leader they must do something. The leader should have done it before now.

A good leader understands that the company wants better leadership. They gave you a guidefor a reason. The leader knows that the manualhas a lot of experience and insights. If they want the task done right away, there must be a reason, and it is essential. It is not always easy to find the time among the leaders' busy schedule; however, they manage to make time to get it done.

Through finishing this task's simple actions, the leader earns the coach and their team's respect. They start to see the good benefits and the impact on the team. The coach continues challenging the leader and makes them a better leader.

It is vital to becoming a good leader. You will see how the team will respect you as their leader. Take all situations head-on. Do not wait until the last minute. Always have a positive attitude and let your team see it.

Exceptional Leadership

Situation One: You have an employee who approaches you with the idea that could help the team. As a leader, you probably should have already done this, but you have not gotten to it.

Being an exceptional leader is hard to achieve. It requires the leader to give more than is asked. That is my you do not find many leaders in this category. With this situation, you will do everything a good leader will do. However, you will also teach and guide them to eventually be a leader. It was an idea brought to you by an employee. Allow that employee to be a direct supervisor of the image with the guidance of the leader. In the military, there is a system called *"Train the Trainer."* It is based on teaching the employees to be leaders so they can be leaders themselves.

Doing this extra work will create a team of employees who can lead and guide the unit when the leader is not around. The leader will no longer have a couple of employees. Instead, they would have a team of leaders.

Situation Two: You are in a meeting that is already very long when an employee asks a hard question. The employee questions the values of the project which are being focused on. The employee askes, *"How did you get to this solution?"* They continue with another question by asking, *"What made all of us decide to do it this way in the first place?"*

As an exceptional leader, a different approach is taken. They will involve the team more. As the questions are asked, the leader will address them directly.

They will explain the reason for the decision, much like a good leader. What sets an exceptional leader apart is they also asked the team for their suggestions and ideas.

The approach of an exceptional leader brings unity within the team. The teams know they will be challenging, and the decisions are made as a team. They understand that the future is in the team's hands, and the conclusions are agreed upon within the group.

Situation Three: The company hires someone on the team that does a job the leader is not familiar with. The leader does not know what is involved in the position. Therefore, they do not know what the keys to success are with the job.

When an exceptional leader is faced with this situation, they see their lack of knowledge for the position. They will add to their daily tasks to sit down with the employee and train them in their job. They will ask questions and learn everything they can about the position and what is involved. The leader is humble enough to know they do not know everything. After they learn about the situation, the leader will create a cross-training program. This will allow everyone on the team to learn about the new position and enable each team member to know for every teamwork.

As a result of the leader spending time with the new employee, they gain a deeper connection. The team sees how the leader is not afraid to work beside them and learn from the group. The leader shows that there is a lot to be learned from each other. As they develop a cross-training system, it allows the position to be filled by anyone on the team if there is an emergency. When someone cannot be available, someone in the group can step up and take charge.

Situation Four: A company thinks the leadership needs a little help. They bring in a coach to help the leaders to improve their leadership. The coach informs a leader they must do something. The leader should have done it before now.

When you finally hit an exceptional leader's status, it is a time to enjoy what you are doing as a mentor, leader, and friend to your team. Even as an exceptional leader, you could use a coach on leadership. The leader recognizes the opportunity for growth. They are not afraid to ask questions. The coach asked you to do the task right away. You complete the job immediately and ask the coach questions to better understand why it needed to be done at that time.

The leader knows this is the time to learn from the coach. They see the result from their hard work and realize they still have a lot to learn. An exceptional leader cares about the growth of their team. They know everything they can and teach their team to be the same. The set the example and guide others to be where they are or better.

Chapter 7: Finding Your Leadership Style and Leading Like a Champ

A smart leader knows how to strategically put his team into place, aligning each step to achieve their goals each time. A leader should understand the essential things theyneed to achieve, and he must know how to communicate this effectively. They also need to represent properly to their company, organization, or team. They need to be able to relate to their subordinates and maintain a healthy relationship with their team.

Leaders are the torch bearers of change and chosen to deliver positive effects to what they represent. An effective leadership strategy is composed of methods and styles which will fit the different personalities of individuals. A comprehensive approach translates objectives into specific actions and delivers outcomes as what is expected.

The leadership role is evolving,where itfocuses more on the results and, more importantly,on the employees' well-being. Here are a few different leadership styles.

Task-Oriented Leadership

A leader of this group focuses and stays with the team until the completion of each task. A task-oriented leader strictly sets out directives and schedules forthe team members to follow and creates specific time frames for eachgoal to be met. They value the importance of completing the task more than building a relationship with their team.

People-Oriented Leadership

This type of leader aims to build a strong and long-lasting relationship with his subordinates. The quality of the relationship is essential in delegating a task and cultivating the work culture. They recognize the importance of the employee's role in achieving more significant results. They use different techniques to make an employee skillfulthrough training, team-building exercises, and open communication between top management and workers.

Supportive Leadership

Leaders using these styles are most often called *"supportive leaders."*In a workplace setting, the head of a team delegates tasks and stays with employees in support until completing tasks. The manager often works with their employees until they are skilled enough on their own and with minimal supervision. This will create authenticity and genuine sincerity of the managers towards the people they work with.

- ➢ Advantages
  - ○ The manager can closely monitor errors that may happen and eradicate it before they continue.
  - ○ Working hand in hand with their employees strengthens the bond and their employees' confidence in them as leaders and what they represent, ultimately reducing the company's turnover rate.
  - ○ This will encourage growth for both the leader and the team through shared knowledge, acquired resources, and by facilitating recommendations and suggestions.
  - ○ This creates further developments of both the leader and the team in terms of emotional growth, intelligence milestones, constructive arguments, and even people's service orientation.
  - ○ By creating a mentor-mentee environment, these employees can turn into future leaders of the industry.
  - ○ Employees can receive the necessary training and supervision in getting a job done, which will also boost their morale in performing their duties.

- ➢ Disadvantages
  - ○ The downside of this strategy is how it takes longer to make an employee skillful.
  - ○ Due to too much closeness, personal boundaries can often be disturbed between the boss and his subordinates.
  - ○ It may become difficult for a boss who is viewed as a friend to reprimand his team and less fire them for being incompetent.
  - ○ Employees may become dependent on their boss and cannot properly function without constant supervision.

Interactive Leadership

Leaders engage employees in task matters by understanding the goals, procedures, and steps. The leader takes into consideration the active participation and recommendations of their employees.

This strategy increases the employee's confidence and participation in a workplace setting through a leader, creating a network of support. This strategy is commonly known as *"shared leadership,"* wherein objectives are shared, creating equally through motivation and commitment. An interaction occurs between the manager and his subordinates, exchanging different sets of ideas, recommendations, and clarifications to get things done. The business builds employee support as a great leader knows how to get involved.

- ➤ Advantages
  - ○ This strategy increases the employees' understanding of the importance of tasks—their roles in attaining the goals, and the essential steps.
  - ○ This strengthens a leader's role by exhibiting themself the quality of a person leading a company to success via influence and proper delegation.
  - ○ Responsibilities are legally distributed to the employees, and each member influences the others.
  - ○ This will allow the employees to be involved in the process and complete a task,making them feel important.
  - ○ Roles are being assigned based on the employee's expertise.
  - ○ Active interaction between a manager and an employee innovates new ideas, creates new opportunities, and heightens a positive relationship between two groups of people.

- ➤ Disadvantages
  - ○ Employees may become over-familiar with their bosses resulting ina blurred relationship once disagreements occur.
  - ○ Consistency may become an issue in the performance of an employee.
  - ○ Ineffective decisions can be created due to the influence of the manager and employee relationship.

There are factors a leader can take into consideration in selecting an effective strategy or style of leadership.

- ➤ A leader must know the kind of people they are leading. They must be aware of their personalities and traits by continuously administering their day-to-day work.
- ➤ A leader must adapt to change and create a sense of acceptance that leadership and learning to collaborative. As theylead, they must also take inputs from the team in their stewardship.
- ➤ He must be open to non-traditional strategies to implement and address various situations using different methods. They must consider the generation and age of their team in selecting a leadership style.
- ➤ They must treat every situation as something unique and must not copy well-established plans of famous leaders as this may not be well suited tothe team.
- ➤ A leader should never be afraid of trying different approachesto leadership.They must be open to criticism and feedback to be able to identify the right method of administration.

> In selecting an effective strategy, a leader must comprehend the value of the goals he needs to achieve and the quality of people he will be working with.

This is how leaders provide directions, create strategies, implement ideas, and encourage employees to finish a designated task.

Autocratic Leadership

In this type of leadership, a leader takes control of the overall decision making and has the complete command of getting things done. The leader takes charge of everything without taking into consideration the employee's input and interests. Team members are expected to comply with the manager's decisions and keep up to their pace.

The best time to practice this kind of style is when the team is on a tight deadline, well-motivated, and has all the needed information to finish the required task. This is also beneficial in completing a short-term, risky project and routinely work with unskilled workers. However, this type of leadership creates a higher turnover rate among employees and lowers employees' morale.

Laissez Faire Leadership

The word *"Laissez Faire"* means let it be as it is the direct opposite of the autocratic way of leading. One famous leader that used this style is the former late United States President Ronald Reagan. He said, *"Surround yourself with the best people you can find, delegate authority, and do not interfere as long as the policy you have decided upon is being carried out."*

"Surround Yourself with the Best People You Can Find, Delegate Authority, and Do Not Interfere as Long as the Policy You Have Decided Upon is Being Carried Out."

The leader allows the employees to participate in the decision-making process while taking responsibility for the consequences. Theytrusttheir employees to perform better with minimal supervision and deliver the job as expected. The manager focuses more on achieving thejob's intellectual and strategic part than emphasizinghis team's actions.

Employees are given the liberty of creating their own decisions related to their work, as they are open to sharing their views and suggestions. Team members who are best to consider in this style are intellectual, self-reliant, possess initiative, loyal, and require minimal supervision. This style maximizes the qualities of the team members and often offers criticism when necessary. The leader picks the right people for the job and allows them to perform well,saving time, and carrying the task faster.

Democratic / Participative Leadership

Members are given the freedom to participate in decision making. Ideas are exchanged freely, and discussion is often held to encourage participation. The members play an essential role indecision making but with the supervision of the leader. The leader serves as the guidance and control of the group. They direct their team members on performing their job well while providing feedback and suggestions to them. This leadership style converts workers into better employees who are motivated and skilled. It creates a working environment of positivity and creativity.

Bureaucratic Leadership

Leaders using this strategy adheres to following the rules and policies set by their organization. They also make sure their subordinates follow the same procedures by obeying the same rules. Employees are often recognized through adherence to their organization's practices.

Public industries are best to practice this kind of relationship since they rely heavily on complying with the rules. An example of a famous bureaucratic leader is former late United States President Winston Churchill. He was known as being difficult to persuade and made sure to carry his plans with perseverance.

A leader in this setting is meticulous and detailed oriented, commonly use in the government-industry.They are strong-minded people as they find the need to keep everything in order and ensure the rules are strictly followed.This efficient rule-based leadership styleis best for organizing, and governing societies with a system created in controlling things such as a department, organization, or company.

Leadership Strategy: Influencing, Engaging, and Encouraging

The various roles of a leader rely mostly on how they influence their people, engage in their work, and encourage them to achieve a common goal. Learning to be a more effective leader is more than just having the capacity to lead but rather how to create quality and valuable employees in the long run.

Influencing: The leader's ability to control is mastery. Influencing others is identified as one of the core leadership skills a leader must possess.

Define and Communicate Vision: A leader's vision is critical for the organization's future. This sets out the path and direction that drives the members to the same purpose. Putting this vision into action must be a priority in achieving specific goals and objectives. The ability to influence a person determines the level of hard work a team member can contribute, performing together under a common goal. A vision will provide direction, set out important goals to achieve, create effective strategies, and measured progress.
To be a significant influencer, one must answer the question, *"where are we going?"*

A leader must be direct, concise, and strategic on his plan in reaching the destination. They must clearly identify the details of what their goals look like.This will enable the team to pinpoint their present progress and develops strategies that could make them closer to their target.

Engaging: The ability of a leader to engage in his employees create great teams, opens new opportunities, and builds relationships that last longer within the group. Employees want to feel valued and appreciated,which gives them a reason for their work to be more productive and produce more significant results. A leader who knows how to engage in his team's daily work through positive criticism and healthy feedback creates a pool of workers who works more than is required and is expected of them.

Encourage recognition: An effective leadership strategy that some managers often neglect can significantly impact an employee's performance. Whether they are big or small, celebrating achievements encourages employees to perform better and creates continued commitment to their mission and visions.

Encouraging: According to John Maxwell,*"People go farther than they thought they could when someone else thinks they can."* There is nothing better than having a boss who knows how to encourage their team than a boss who gets things donein a more challenging way.

People Go Further Than They Thought They Could When Someone Else Thinks They Can.

One of the main reasonsemployees last longer in a company relies on upper management to their subordinates. A great leader knows how to focus on their team members' strengths and drives these abilities into motivation and better work performance. Helping individuals turning a less powerful statement of *"I can't"* into a more powerful messageof*"I will"* is an example of employee's results from encouragement. To these, a leader must, this is a must.

➢ **Delegate and Empower**: Empowering team members by giving them greater responsibility is an effective way of leading. This will provide them with a sense of self-worth and importance. A leader must delegate areas for his members to focus on and trust them enough to finish the job. A person is a social being that thrives through recognition and responsibility. Create an open communication line to them by building rapport and facilitating an available network of suggestions and feedback.

To commit to continued excellence, a leader must pursue to strive for constant growth and learning. Leadership is a process and evolves in every possible way and time. A leader must quickly adapt to change and innovation to create progress. They must commit to developingtheir skills for leadership as the most critical function of management. A leader must drive for results of excellencethrough aligning their values and goals.

Leadership Branding

A leadership brand is something a leader has that represents their leadership style and the business. This is every leader's identity, which differentiates them from other leaders. It is commonly based on their values as a person and set of ideals they believe in. This is cultivated on how they perceive people based on their experience and relationship with them.

For instance, if a person is tasked to lead a team and they believe controlling things will get things done more comfortably and faster, thus, he poses a strict ruler and expect people to follow them with no exceptions. Some leaders believe getting involved in his member's work is vital for achievement, then they lead by encouraging their team members to participate. All brands of leadership vary from one another but are essential in accomplishing goals.

Most leaders carry their own brands as they approach different work challenges.Leaders use different approaches in leading a team of people and defining a solution to a specific job. They align themselves with the needs of the situation and the kind of people they are over.

Branding is vital as it creates an impression and leaves a mark on a target audience. A brand sets the tone of what an employee expects from their leader and from their company.

Since a leadership brand is the leader's identity, they need to carry themselves through actions and thoughts. In most cases, when a leader takesa leader's effort, they also cultivate future leaders. It is something a leader can offer that makes them a better choice for an exceptional leader.

Here are some steps leaders can take in creating their own leadership brand.

- ➢ Leaders must identify and establish their objectives and how to accomplish them while putting their stakeholders' interests.
- ➢ They must always be authentic and should not copy someone else's brand.
- ➢ Clarify and identify what they want to be known for and help them develop the right approach in spearheading a team. For instance, you want to be known as a leader with honesty and integrity or open-minded leadership.
- ➢ Focuses more on their unique traits, andthey will be pulled into roles that fit their talents.
- ➢ Point out catchy phrases to describe him as a leader, such as *"Innovative Manager"* or *"Friendly Manager."*This is based on their approach to leadership and personal values.
- ➢ Creating their own vision as a leader and coming up with a statement withtheir objectives.

A leader needs to convey their leadership's thoughts through actions and results. This will serve as the basis for how employees perceive their boss as a leader. It is also essential for a leader to reflect their priorities and their values on their leadership branding. Otherwise, a leader does not seem to portray an authentic representation of their promises or acts contradictory to their values, then their leadership brand could derail. Putting more focus on the authenticity of what a leader is and tries to help them produce significant results and open more opportunities.

Leaders should acknowledge the need for continued learning and growth.Creating a well-known, successful leadership brand comes with years of perseverance and a handful of experience. Results can be achieved after successful branding is established.

Chapter 8: The Qualities, Skills, and Traits to be The Best of The Best

It does not matter if you are a new leader or have been in a leadership role for several years. Everyone wants to know and understand what some qualities of an exceptional leader are.

I will open your mind to such traits, skills, and qualities you must consider. These will help you to become a better leader. Many of these leaders today tend to forget about it. While some of them, you may think it is common sense. Others may catch your eye because you did not know of them.

Being Self-Motivated

Sometimes it is hard to be motivated. If you are not motivated, you cannot boost your team. Dig deep inside you and find out what motivates you. For example, what motivates me to work hard is my family. I do everything for them, and they mean the world to me.

Take pride in everything you do. Have a passion for your work. This pride and passion will help bring the motivation you need. No one will follow you if you are not motivated to do it. Show your team you are motivated and will be inspired as well.

You will find that if you are motivated, your team will be motivated, and you and your team will exceed expectations.

Have High Standards

As a leader, you want your team to hold high standards. You take pride in your work. That work needs to show your pride. This does not mean you keep your team to high standards, and you do not need to meet them. An exceptional leader sets the standard. That means, if you expect your team to hold those standards, you must exceed them—leader by example. Show them what your bar is that everyone must follow.

Do not set standards so hard that it is impossible to uphold them. You can have high standards, yet you must make them reasonable. If your standards are so high that it is impossible to achieve them, you set your team up for failure. I saw this all the time in the military. Some leaders would never be happy with the work you would do. No matter how hard you tried, you could never meet their standard. For example, you have old equipment that has been in your company for over 10 years. Your leader wants it looking like new. Yet, it shows wear and tears for many years.

Confidence

Some people think that you either have or do not have confidence. What do you think? I used to think it was this way. I have a different thought about trust now. I feel it is something that can be learned.

Your confidence is your perception of what you can do in a specific role. It is built through your experiences in life. For example, when a person first joins the military, they are nervous. They are unsure of their abilities. They are not sure if they can repeal down a wall. They are scared to low crawl under barbwire with live bullets flying over their heads. The lack the confidence to do these things. Yet they do it! The more they do it and practice, the more confident they become.

When I first joined the military, I never really fired a rifle. I lacked the confidence in my marksmanship. During range week, we spent all day for a week on the range firing my rifle. Within the time, I gained confidence. By the end of the week, I was so confident with my rifle that I hardly ever got anything less than an expert. There was always one that got away, and I would hit 39 out of 40 every time.

Based on my experience in the military, my thoughts changed. I now know that confidence is learned and not given to you. Eleanor Roosevelt said it best when she said, *"You gain strength, courage, and confidence by every experience in which you really stop to look fear in the face."*

You Gain Strength, Courage, and Confidence by Every Experience in which You Really Stop to Look Fear in the Face."

Show Your Positivity and Optimism

We are not always going to get the best jobs to do. Sometimes, there are tasks we will not like or enjoy. Your team may think of these jobs a punishment. This can be a difficult task to be optimistic about. However, it is essential to show your optimism and be confident about the charges.

When you see someone laughing, do you want to laugh? You may not know what they are laughing about, yet you start to laugh. Laughter is contagious, and so is positivity. If you are optimistic about the task, your team will be as well.

Always remember, you are being watched. Leaders are still under the spotlight. You do not know who is watching. It could be your team, supervisor, or a regular customer. Therefore, it is always important to be optimistic about every task.

You are Accountable

Leaders are given so many responsibilities. The outcome of each of these is not always right. Sometimes they are wrong. What do you do? Do you blame someone on the team? Exceptional leaders take control and accept the outcome. They do not play the blame game a hold themselves responsible.

Think about it, if you do not hold yourself accountable and you blame others, you become the victim. Victims are not leaders. An exceptional leader is there for their team. If they mess up on a task, you take responsibility for the outcome. It was your job as the leader to ensure they were appropriately trained. If they did something that shows they needed better training, it is ultimately the leader's responsibility. It is not that of the team member because they were only doing what they have been taught.

Be Courageous

A great philosopher, Aristotle, said courage is the first of all the virtues. He said this because all the others are not possible without courage. A leader must have courage because of the decisions they make. Sometimes, these decisions will be unpopular, and your team will not like them.

Learn to trust and confide in your team. Be willing to try new things without fear of the outcome. Be sure to take issues head-on, and do not leave them unresolved. Robert Louis Stevenson said it best when he said, *"keep your fears to yourself but share your courage with others."*

Keep Your Fears to Yourself, but Share Your Courage with Others

Be Engaged with Your Team

No, this does not mean you get engaged or married to your team. Keep focused on the tasks. It does not matter how busy you are. You must interact side-by-side with your team to complete tasks. Do not be on the sidelines as a lousy supervisor. I refer to them as supervisors because they are not leaders. Do not be afraid to get your hands dirty with your team.

Several years ago, my family and I loved going to an outstanding buffet-style restaurant. While we were eating, the manager comes over to ask how the food was and if we needed anything. He even noticed my drink was empty. He asked what I was drinking and brought me a new glass. He did not need to do that. He could have told the waitress, or I could have gotten it myself. I noticed it was not only our table. He did it with everyone. That is the perfect example of an engaging leader. Even his interaction with the staff reflected this. He took pride in who works for him and the service offered.

Think About Your Character

Think about the type of person you are. What is your personality or character? Leaders are one of a kind. They have a unique persona. For example, a retired soldier, a veteran, or has served for any amount of time puts off a specific persona. It is easy to look at someone and tell if they have served in the military. No, it is not because of their haircut. Yet, that does help. It is the way they carry themselves.

You Need to Have a Sense of Humor

This can be one of the hardest things for a leader. Especially if you are new to having a leadership role. You want others to take you seriously. Some leaders have a desire to be a perfectionist. This causes them to be too critical and judge themselves and others hard.

Being a perfectionist as a leader is setting you and your team up for failure. You must realize if something could go wrong, it will. There is no such thing as perfection.

Stop taking life seriously. Learn to laugh at your mistakes. Do not laugh at your team for their mistakes but laugh with them. Show them it is ok to make mistakes and work together to fix them.

Bring Passion to What You Do

Exceptional leaders are passionate about their job. They want to see their team grow and become leaders. They want to always be moving forward in their career. Your passion will affect your team. When you are passionate, it will bring energy and love within the group. You and your team become a force to be reckoned with and can accomplish anything. Steve Jobs said, *"You have to be burning with an idea, or a problem, or a wrong that you want to right. If you are not passionate enough from the start, you will never stick it out."*

If You Are Not Passionate Enough from the Start, You Will Never Stick It Out.

Have Integrity and Be Ethical

Be honest in everything you do. No one likes a leader who is always dishonest. Your strong values will become a critical part of your leadership. They will guide you to make the right decisions. Everything you do will reflect your values and help you become more ethical in your team's findings.

Your Emotions Make a Difference

Understanding your own emotions can be challenging. Try understanding the feelings of your team. You must have a handle of your emotions. There is more to it than just understanding them. You must know how they affect your team and those around you. Once you have this understanding, it makes it easier to control them.

Having control of your emotions will help you stay calm and make it easier to make the right decisions. Your feelings have a significant impact on the outcome of your decision. With emotional control, you will gain so much more. Charles Swindoll said, *"Life is 10% of what happens to me and 90% of how I react tc it."*

Life is 10% of What Happens to Me and 90% of How I React to It.

Have Humility

Everyone has had a leader who thinks everything that happens is becoming of them. They do not give credit to the ones who made them shine. Where is the humility in that?

On the road to becoming an exceptional leader, you must be humble. Start focusing on what your team needs and take their feedback to heart. Henri Frederic Amiel said, *"There is no respect for others without humility in one's self."* This is so true. If you are not humble, you cannot get the respect of your team.

There is No Respect for Others Without Humility in One's Self.

Be Disciplined

This is an attribute that every leader should have. Sadly, some leaders lack it. Discipline is not about rewards and punishments. It is about your leadership. It is about your self-control. It is about your inner calm. It is about the outer resolutions. Attributes to look at are your willpower and determination to get things done.

Having Risk and Time Management

Your time is valuable. Having good time management is essential for you to get everything accomplished that needs to be finished. Just as your time is precious, so are the risks that may be involved.

In the military, every training exercise requires the leader to complete a risk management worksheet. Risk management has three main areas. Those areas are identifying the risk, evaluating the risk, and addressing the threat. There is a famous saying that they say with the stock market, *"there is no reward, without risk."* There will be some risks you will stay away from while others will be beneficial to your team.

Be an Effective Teacher

We are always learning as a leader. However, you need to be able to share your knowledge with your team. You must become an effective teacher and learn how to communicate your understanding. This falls under training for your team. You are the one who would be providing the training.

Trust Your Team

You expect your team to trust you. In return, you should trust your team. It works both ways. If you do not have this trust, your team will eventually fall apart. Sometimes it takes work on the part of everyone in the group. However, it starts with you as their leader. Show them you have trust in your team, and they will give you trust in return.

Keep in mind, the quickest way to show you do not trust your team is through micromanaging. Stay away from this if you want your team to trust you.

Evaluate Your Team

This does not mean you are keeping tabs on your team. You want them to grow and progress in their career. Evaluating your team members allows you to get to know them better. Focus on their strengths and improvements. Never consider their improvements as weaknesses. Always point out their strengths. For each area that needs improvement, include their power in that area and plan to work on the site to elevate that area and make your team member a better person. Allow them to have a say in the decision-making process.

You may think this is a long list of traits and skills already. The truth, it is only a handful of the many gifts that you need as a leader. The list could go on and on. Leaders are always working hard to perfect this list, and it would be impossible to list them all. Search within you and evaluate your leadership skills and find cut what makes you the leader you are. Become a great or exceptional leader. Focus on your strengths and learn from your mistakes. Turn your weaknesses into strengths.

Chapter 9: Strategies to Make You Exceptional

Leadership is critical yet essential in any management position. It plays a vital role in the success and downfall of an organization or a company. In managing a workplace, leaders need to represent their company's overall business and create their industry's future. Often, a leader's role is challenging and always on the hot spot for critics and accountabilities. Still, nevertheless, a leader can bring change to the smallest count of individuals to many people.

The primary characteristics of great leaders include:

> - **Know how to create a more excellent vision by setting out a clear and direct path of its** or organization's future.
> - **Influencer:** know how to inspire, motivate, and encourage their people to achieve the objectives.
> - **Display honesty and integrity:** being consistently honest in both successes and failures.
> - **Confident:** always maintain a positive outlook and presents themself in a presentable manner.
> - **A man of action:** a person who translated his words into actions.

The Role of a Leader

In this fast-changing world, the definition of leadership also evolves. Leaders are now expected to adapt quickly to the world's unprecedented pace and continuous modernization. Traditional methods no longer work since new hires become more affluent to technology, giving them more liberty to information.

Present leaders in all organizations and industries cope with the role's pressure since it becomes more challenging to lead than non-millennial leaders.Leaders of today's generation are facing problems wherein previous headliners never encountered them before. Extraordinary results seem superficial and unreachable, given today's challenges. A leader's role becomes too risky for anybody to fill in since the stakes are high, and employees demand more.

How can a leader stay ahead of their pace and prepare themselves to become ready for the role? How can you prepare yourself to embark on the journey of leadership? What are the things you need to possess for you to become the best leader you can be?

Becoming a Leader: The Journey to the Top

An excellent leader often starts from the bottom and work their way up. They begin their journey from being a simple worker having the desire to claim a top management spot. This happens if you purposely follow the rules, produce more significant results, and work more than you were expected. The stories of this journey to the top vary from different individuals. People may find they are drawn to the position because of family lineage, yet some toil their way up.

Often, others believed that some roles are meant for a person to fill in, and sometimes a leadership role suddenly materializes and steers towards them unexpectedly. This scenario is possible due to peer pressure. However, plenty of people are usually attracted to a higher position despite other people's doubts,so they find themselves applying for the job.

Regardless of the journey,everyone embarks on this journey and the reason for them to fill in the role, each leader faces the same impending challenges that come with the position. The only factor they can control is the way they react and respond to the challenge.

Leadership and Change

Change is in conjunction with leadership. The difference is the only constant thing in the world of leadership. Harry S. Truman said, *"Progress occurs when courageous, skillful leaders seize the opportunity to change things for the better."* True leaders know how to transform change into better results.

Progress Occurs when Courageous, Skilful Leaders Seize the Opportunity to Change Things for the Better

In the modern workplace, change is in the form of modernization, technology innovation, employees' access to information, and leadership styles. In all sorts of ways, change is inevitable, particularly in every business industry and organization. Yet change is necessary for management positions. For instance, understanding the modern era of new hires and fresh graduates determines the kind of workers a company can have. Due to media and technology influence, employees become aggressive in selecting their work, making them more demanding and overconfident. This is an example of change's fallback in terms of leadership, yet there are instances that modern employees work better than traditional ones. For example, a stylish set of employees are more familiar with the technology that management can save time and budget for training.

In today's world,it is full of moving parts, the competition in the workplace is also progressing. Recruiting the right people for the job is becoming more complicated than before. Employees expect more of an interactive working environment and would instead not work in a traditional setting.

A good manager must know how to adapt to change and approach different types of people. He must be willing to cope with the evolving workforce. He must know how to come up with a strategic plan to develop his leadership skills and align them with the generation of the team they are leading.

Nowadays, leadership styles that have command and control no longer work with the new set of employees. With technology advancement, significant results are seen more on innovative leaders who know how to develop and emphasize leadership's importance in every organization's level. They use collaboration, giving more emphasis to employee participation, and creating a more collaborative environment wherein employees feel free to share their ideas and be part of the process.

Change in the Workplace

Change happens in the workplace in mainly two areas: internally and externally.Internal factors belong to the workforce, wherein change occurs in the attitude and personalities of an employee. The philosophy of millennial employees compare to non-millennial ones are distinguishable. Technology plays a significant influence on how a millennial works. The need to look for a safer and open working environment to work for is their topmost priority. While on the other hand, the traditional workforce focuses on producing results and are less driven by the modernization. These different individuals' attitudes will contribute to the company's status, both positively and negatively.

Regarding external change, it comprises natural factors such as technology modernization and globalization, economic status, and environmental factors.These are factors surfaces due to natural causes.

As the world progresses, the need for effective and efficient leaders are also moving. The organization can no longer afford to have traditional and outdated leaders leading the modern business. Instead, they invest in developing their people's leadership skills by providing adequate training, high-technology advancements, and making superiors focus more on individuals to make jobs done more comfortably and faster.

Modern Leadership Skills: People Skills

Leaders should develop their people skills that harness their involvement with their teams' works. They must address the changing workforce through more collaborative and open relationshipswith their subordinates. Building relationshipsis essential for an organization's leader, producing coherent workers, good employees, and motivated people to havemore extraordinary achievements.

Modern Leadership Skills: Flexibility

A leader must also develop his flexibility skills, which is a sought-out skill, traditional or not. Leaders must survive the business and his people; a flexib e leader knows how to ride the changing leadership course to provide consistent outcomes.

Modern Leadership Skills: Thinking Ahead

Also, to combat the economy's growth, a leader must always be prepared to shift strategies and mindset based on the situation needed. He must think ahead of others and plan things that may challenge him before they even occur.

Modern Leadership Skills: Participative Management

To address the demand of workers to be involved more, managers must decide to be affected by these decisions.In this case, employees may feel involved and more listened to, resulting in better outcomes and low turnover rates.

The concept in today's leaders is to have people follow them because they want to and not because they must. More directive leaders are now turning into more passive leaders.

Modern Leadership Skills: Self-Leadership

Modern-day workers are more independent than any other generation. They are self-reliant, self-driven, and have access to almost anything. They are too focused on themselves. Hence they are capable of individual work in working as a team. They adopt a wide range of change like the evolution of media and technology;thus, they are valuable to become future leaders.

However, they respond more to a much different style of leadership than the traditional manner. Contradictory to the command and rule of previous leaders, millennial workers focus more on the attitude of leaders who they can relate to.They look for leaders who can aggregate diversity and collaboration to produce significant results. They cooperate more if they were given more responsibility, and they build more responsibly using intellect, technology innovation, creativity, etc.

A new set of leaders must possess this self-criteria to become more qualified for leading a modern team. They must create a working environment like the changing world to go along with the trends.

Modern Leadership Skills: Systematic Leadership

An effective leader knows how to make use of modern technology to produce more efficient results. To become familiar withthe system-driven system, operators will need leaders to be more efficient. By creating a balance between technology and human interaction, a company will turn business into profits.

Modern Leadership Skills: Articulating Change

Articulation is the clarity of delivering what you say. It is a skill difficult to master and tricky to learn. It is developed over time with experience, and leaders who know how to deliver words with clarity creates a vast difference to an audience.

For example, former United States President Barack Obama delivers his speeches to the people with clarity and confidence, communicating his words with power, which creates a lot of meaning. The importance of a successful speech delivery ignited people's trustin a leader, and delivering the words they speak is a bonus.

A great leader knows how to communicate appropriately and confident enough to interpret those words into actions.

Modern Leadership Skills: Leadership Combustor

As the world progresses at a different pace, a new type of leader will emerge.The competition will arise among leaders in terms of qualifications and competencies of the job. Greater demand for high standard leaders with exceptional experience will rise among from another company's needs. A well-prepared leader who knows how to combat innovation and diversity tops the search list.

Forthese individuals to become in-depth and a well-versed leader, the following can be an observe:

> ➢ Heighten your educational attainment; a post-graduate degree becomes more qualified than a person with minimal education.
> ➢ Participate in leadership programs that offer specialization in connection to the world's demand.
> ➢ Engage in workshops that enhance your creativity, learning, skills,and so on as it will become useful in leading people.
> ➢ Try working out your conversation skills. A leader with strong personality skills knows how to talk with people.
> ➢ Continue to update yourself with the latest happenings, such as global trends, technology advancement, and business development. Be equipped with things concerning your industry.

These integrators are factors considered essential to become more efficient and effective leaders. Since change remains constant in this world, leaders need to adapt and innovate to produce consistent results.

Modern Leadership Skills: Characteristics of a Leader

Characteristics are the features of an individual as a person in nature. These are the qualities that made up a person and what makes him something different from others. Usually, these qualities are based on a person's beliefs, educational learnings, and upbringing.

A good leader possesses excellent character. How they treat and lead people reflectstheirpersonality as a person. How they act in the presence of people and when they are not around also defining his character. Integrity and honesty are factors people should look for in a great leader.

Here are some of the commonly encountered characteristics of a good leader and their importance.

Displays a grander vision:A great leader isa visionary leader, one that can envision the future of the business they are doing with great wisdom and imagination. Among the list of characters, the innovative quality is something that every leader should have. A great leader knows how to set a cohesive goal for their team. They focus on and knows how to interpret these goals into results.

Visionary leaders should have the capacity to create a vision that draws teams together and becomesunited in providing coherent positive outcomes. They must create an image alignedwith the company's values and business. They must direct a group according to the task given by delegating specific responsibilities per their qualification. They also must learn how to create a strategic plan to pursue the visions laid ahead.

A great leader has a clear idea of what the business's futureshould look like, create concrete steps, and lead a team to transcribe these visions to life.

Articulation mastery: An effective leader is also a great speaker. An okay verse speech is what mostly keeps a leader famous and influential. Most well-known leaders are great in delivering speeches such as Barack Obama, Bill Clinton, and Steve Jobs. Being able to speak well makes a leader a significant influencer. Through the power of words, they can inspire, motivate, and become a catalyst for change for people who needed a pushover.

Since the leader represents the company's business, they need to develop the articulation of words to communicate its goals. They also need to display the maximum clarity of communication, ensuring the following: the comments are in line with the appropriate vision of the company, ignite enthusiasm and inspiration for the team, reflect the culture and values they represent, encourage participation, and communicate with clarity through actions.

It will be challenging to become a great leader without becoming a great communicator.

Maintains integrity:A leader with excellent character is measured through his virtue. A strong leader is honest, trustworthy, and reliable. Their nature is defined by their actions with and without the presence of people.

They value loyalty from the people they lead becausethey are trustworthy and act for their liabilities and the team's accountability.

Assertive: Is the ability to express strong feelings without being aggressive.It is being confident of performing their responsibilities with less supervision and deliveringtheir vision successively through clear direction to the team.

Assertiveness is expressing honest and direct thoughts, ideas, and feelings without being perceived as loud or arrogant. It does not involve violating the team members' rights, or humiliating them when giving commands and orders, contradictory to being aggressive.

Assertive managers create an honest and authentic relationship with their employees. They express their feelings without making any confrontation and being open to their mistakes without potential conflict.

Walk the talk: There is nothing worse than a person who only talks yet shows no actions. The measurement of being an effective and efficient leader is through the efforts they make. For instance, a country president is criticized for the projects they build and the amount of economy's difference they contribute to,makingthem a better president.

The term itself translates a leader into ensuring their actions match the words they speak. Leading by example, is the most significant indication of a healthy, powerful, and effective leader. It means that leaders immerse themselves in carrying out their vision to the team by drifting out of their comfort zone and carry the task well at the end.

Walking the talk does not only limit you to getting the job done. It also involves simple acts that display respect, integrity, and empathy to the team, thingssuch as lending a hand when things go wrong, being held accountable for the team's mistakes, providing equal treatment to all members, practicing respectful courtesies, and giving freedom of expression without cutting them off.

Creates an environment for growth:A great leader grows along with the team. They build and transform the group as well as making progress themself.

Leadership growth is mandatory, and a leader who remains stagnant falls behind.

Creating an environment that is open for change is an appropriate condition for growth. A functional leader knows how to create an atmosphere where the members can strive to grow and become better individuals. There are various ways on how a manager can make a conducive place of growth for their employees.

> - Create similar values and visions for every team member to follow.
> - Enhance the potential skill set of all team members for growth and development.
> - Motivate the team to perform at their best.
> - Create memorable and shared experiencesfor solving problems to become the igniter of future resolutions.
> - Challenge everyone to takethemselves out of their comfort zone.
> - Construct a desirable future for everyone to focus on.
> - Provide feedback and open communication.

There are countless things a leader can do to improve the members of their team. Leadership is an exciting journey for a passionate leader, strives to create a difference, and educate people with valuable knowledge. Given the appropriate training and equipped with practical leadership skills, a leader can do so much and can do better.

Ability to delegate:A leader is not supposed to do all the work alone as a part of being an effective team leader is knowing how to distribute the workload to the right members. Delegation of tasks and responsibilities is essential to avoid overwork and burnout. Delegation aid with the skills development of a member in completing a task. For instance, they learn how to become more independent and develop new skills such as initiative and creativity. This will enable them to become skillful in future projects and eventually turn out to become leaders as well.

Practice self-gratitude:A part of self-development is self-growth. Nothing is better than a leader who knows how to appreciate the milestone and be grateful for every opportunity they are given. Practicing self-gratitude is being thankful for what a person has and the things that surround them. A grateful leader radiates this positivism to others and applies it to the way theyleadthe team.

Empathy: This is a practice of relatingto the way others feel and their shortcomings. A good leader knows how to comfort their team when necessary and how to steer away for privacy. Showing empathy is like showing a leader cares, which is a critical leadership skill.

Modern Leadership Skills: Challenges of Being a Leader

The decision to accept the challenge of being a leader comes with added responsibility, which seems more challenging at first glance. Pressure, difficult people, culture issues, and many more are part of the package in leading a team and are inevitable. The leader's responsibility is to cope with these challenges, internal and external, to create effective strategies to combat these circumstances. Here are some of the many challenges a leader faces.

Becoming disconnected from the team: Relationship between the head of the team and its members varies and can change. What started strong at first can turn sour overnight. Disagreement can fall sometimes, and a close relationship of a leader to their team can become more contractual and detached. It is due to leaders isolating themselves from their colleagues, which creates a feeling of disconnection and loneliness. A good leader knows how to administer orders and commands while maintaining a healthy relationship with their subordinates.

Struggling to establish complete authority: One of the challenges a leader can face is to fill in a shoe left by the previous leader. Being compared to someone who made a significant impact on the company can lead to self-doubts and anxiety.

Lack of problem-solving skills:A great asset of a leader solves problems. The skills to analyze, come up with a solution, and resolve the issueare problem-solving skills. A functional leader knows how to deal with issues effectively.

Identity shift: There are instances that a leader may have become a recent mother, father, or adjusting to a new role. Switching in this role might become a challenge for a leader, making it challenging to provide the right persona to the job.For some, it is overwhelming that they end up compromising two different roles.

A leader must require themself a time off if necessary, adjust to a new role and shift to leading people promptly. Theyneed to develop self-awareness and ask for help if things get out of control. Doing so does not make him less of a leader but rather more of a human being who cannot control things.

A leader must learn how to shift into these roles by focusing on his priorities, attitudes, and developing a new skillset toeffectively manage a team.

Micro-managing people: The worst thing a leader can do is to micro-manage their team members. Not delegating tasks prevail for employees to grow and enhance their creativity. Micromanagement is considered to have a negative effect, as it takes away freedom and creativity. It does not give employees the chance to display trust to their leader, for it practically dictates their actions.

Leaders should be the opposite of micro-managers; a leader must have faith in the employee by giving them enough responsibility and positively criticizing them.

Leadership pressure: Taking the role of being a leader is not just a walk in the park and eating ice cream; aside from the challenges, there is also leadership pressure. There are moments when a leader cannot cope with the required hard work per their role. There are plenty of factors that cause this pressure; for instance, managers expect too much from the team supervisors to deliver unhampered results, create a short budget strategy, or havetime constraints. If this happens, it will generate a surge of panic for the leaders, causing them to become ineffective and incompetent.

Strong leaders know how to combat pressure without showing signs of panic and frustrations. They can compose themself to focus on the problem and create a strategy to resolve it.

Chapter 10: Strengthen in Your Leadership Abilities

Leadership is essential to any organization. They depend on their leaders to mold the company. As a leader, you are always striving to improve and creating impressive results. It is a continuous learning process. Exceptional leaders are incredibly skilled in five areas of management. Every leader has at least some of these areas in them.

Great Communication Skill

Exceptional leadership goes together with outstanding communication. For you to be an effective leader, you must know how to communicate effectively. You are trusted by the organization to lead your team. How are you supposed to do this? It is easy, learn to talk to them. Always keep them informed and listen to any type of feedback. Sometimes, you will have a variety of different team members who perform variouskinds of jobs. You must provide communication for each of these different positions. Clear instructions for your team will increase efficiency and productivity and more positive results.

I have seen many leaders forget about nonverbal communication. This form of communication says a lot about effective communication. Be aware of the words you say, the tone you say those words, and your body language. Your focus should be on clarity and sensitivity for your team. Learn to always speak clearly, truthfully, and concisely. Do not beat around the bush. Get to the point and be specific.

Exceptional Time Management

Every leader needs to have time management. This is more than managing your time. It also involves prioritizing tasks and getting organized. Would you want a leader who is not organized? Each task that is on your schedule should have a set amount of time set aside. This is considered time management for those tasks. It is also essential to complete each task in the time you set aside for it. If you do not, that means you would need to place more time later,and you may not complete the task by the due date.

Detractions can be a killer of your time management. Therefore, many leaders will also plan for unexpected distractions when planning their schedules.

For example, I have a friend who does several different jobs. He works as a teacher part-time during the days. He teaches children in China, Japan, and around the world throughout the night. Finally, he is also a freelance writer, where sometimes he has any number of projects going on at once. Sometimes it is only one. Other times it is over 10. Each project has a deadline. His online teaching also has lessons to create, evaluations on the students, anda 25 to 50-minute class. His part-time education sometimes has meetings, assignments to grade, testing, etc. That seems like a lot to handle. Without adequate time management, it would be impossible. What he did was create a schedule in excel. He blocked out his scheduled classes for his nighttime teaching. Each type is 50 minutes. He recorded when his office hour is each week when he will do evaluations and grade assignments. He also records meetings and appointments. Yes, you could do all this with google calendar, but for him, it is easier to see it on excel. This gives him a chance to see what is going on and when each thing will be done.

Like my friend, it is essential to have a schedule that is planned out. As I talked to him about it, he also told me that he plans extra time for each slot to give time for things to get done. I looked at his schedule and asked him if he sleeps. He told me it is right here. Yes, he plans that on the list too. He even plans personal time with his family. He is so busy, no wonder he needs such a schedule. If you noticed, I did not mention freelance writing. Do not worry. It is there. He figures out how much time needed for each project to give him time to finish a project and hit the due date.

Organizational Awareness

An exceptional leader will always have organizational awareness. There are so many different types of structures within an organization. It is essential for you to know and understand all of them—most organizations of leadership hierarchy. You find a great example of this within the military. The senior management is given an enormous task that involves several different departments to complete. They send parts of the missionfor each team that specializes in that area. Each group does not see the big picture. However, as a leader of the team, you must know the bigger picture. This way, when your team is complaining or question the task, you can answer them.

One of the biggest things for you to understand is the organization's teams' structure and command chain. With this knowledge, you will have a great understanding of the organization and you as a leader.

Problem Solving

Problem-solving skills are essential to every leader. You will always be faced with issues and problems within your team. Sometimes, other leaders may come to you for advice on a problem. You must learn this skill to be an effective leader. This is not a skill that just comes to you. It is realized with experience and time. At a minimum, you should know the following key points and understand them.

- ➢ **Be proactive:** Do not wait for new issues or problems to arise. Look for them. Find them. Have a solution to solve the issue before it becomes a significant concern later. Do not wait!
- ➢ **Define what the problem is clearly:** Have a clear objective or solution for solving the issue. Create a way to succeed.
- ➢ **Analyze the issues:** You will want to be as detailed as possible. Look at all sides of the problem. Find any variables that may help you to understand the cause of the issue.
- ➢ **Create an awareness:** You will want to be aware of every solution possible. Think about the pros and cons of each solution. Do not be afraid to obtain the input of your team. Significantly if the issue or the answer will affect them.
- ➢ **Select the solution that is best:** You have found all these solutions. Choose one of the solutions that you feel would give the best outcome.
- ➢ **Put your solution in play:** Inform your team of the solution and execute it. This is where your leadership skills start to shine. As you and your team perform the answer, look for flaws or additional issues, and adjust accordingly to make it work and see success.
- ➢ **Pause and reflect:** Look at your leadership and problem-solving skills. Evaluate your strengths and weaknesses. Take note of your weaknesses and look at them as things you can improve on. There is always something that you could do better. If your team helped with the solution, you can reflect on them and let them know what they did well and what you could work on together. This gives you a chance to train them to become an exceptional leader.

Exceptional Leadership

This is a no brainer. Considering this book is about leadership. Combining all the skills you have been learning in this book will help you become an exceptional leader. It will also help you develop your team to become outstanding leaders as well.

Stay positive during the time you are a leader. Show your problem-solving skills and continue to advance your career—know-how and when to delegate responsibility to your team. Allow them a chance to lead a task. Evaluate how they do and meet with them to further develop them as the organization's future leaders.

In the military, the leaders have monthly counseling for all the soldiers in their squad. They evaluate their performances. This includes what they did well on and what they need to improve. They also develop a growth plan. This allows for each leader to help their team grow and strengthen their weaknesses. It is the same strategy for leaders in an organization. You must continue to communicate with your team, so they plan to grow as a leader and an individual.

Chapter 11: Tough Challenges Organizationswith Leadership

There is one thing every organization has in common all over the world. They face challenges. The leadership which runs each organization sees these challenges and must make hard decisions. These decisions will affect the future of the organization. Deep in the heart of an organization is the type of leadership they have.

Real leadership is based on three basic needs. First, they need to be honest in all their doings. The leaders represent the organization, their team, and who they are. Second, they need authenticity. They need to stay true to themselves and not genuinely being someone they are not. That means do not try to mimic how others leader. Be yourself and lead the way you know best. First, create meaningful relationships with your team. These relationships create a family atmosphere at work. When you have a relationship with your team, they are more likely to give more for the team's benefits.

I am not saying it is easy. In fact, it takes work to become an exceptional leader. You must know how to serve your team and their needs, inspire them to give everything they have, and 110%, guiding them to be excellent at what they do. You want to take pride in your leadership and your team. You want your team to take pride in having an exceptional leader and the work they give for you.

With that said, there will be times when you meet a roadblock. Sometimes, the task seems entirely impossible. What separates a bad, fair, and exceptional leader is the way you look at these roadblocks. It is like asking the age-old question, *"is the glass half full, or is it half empty?"*

Is the Glass Half Full, or Is it Half Empty?

"Is the glass half empty?" Do you see this roadblock impossible? When you think of it as half empty, you are setting yourself and your team up for failure. You do not see any chance of improvement. Eventually, that glass will be emptied.

"Is the glass half full?" Do you see a chance to improve yourself and your team? Every challenge allows learning. You can find new strengths and skills you never knew you had. Eventually, you full the other half of the glass and find that it is now full of new knowledge.

You set the tone for the way you look at each challenge. Exceptional leaders are always learning and see *the glass half full."* Throughout this chapter, I will talk about different leadership challenges. I want you to think about your own leadership style and the way your team looks at you. How do these challenges relate to your leadership?

Self-Challenges: Challenges from Within

One of the biggest challenges you will face in leadership is yourself. That is right! You will meet many different challenges. This may be due to various reasons.

Do not get me wrong. Many obstacles will come into your path from the outside world. Regardless of what forces from the world jump out in front of you, your feelings, thoughts, and reactions are the biggest challenges. Therefore, what are some of the forces within yourself that may hold you back from your true leadership potential?

Humility: Being humble as a leader may seem easy. You may even look at me and saying, *"really?"* You work hard, and things always work out. You get praise from your own leadership and how well you are doing. You start to believe all the hype of your success. You start feeling it is all becomes of you. You think all credit is yours to behold. Do you see where I am going? Where is humility? Do you want to be on a team with that type of leader? This type of leader does not give credit to those who deserve the credit.

I have seen many bad and great leaders. The best of the best are those who have humility. They have an understanding that leadership is not about glory or authority. They impart and influence their team. The most successful leaders know who deserves real recognition. They value their team.

Humility can be a challenge for leaders. However, it a quality worth fighting for to achieve.

Self-Confidence: In all my travels, I have noticed another common factor in many leaders. They struggle with doubting themselves. It is funny. The more a leader succeeds, the more they suspect. You would not think it was that way. Yet, it is true! Successful leaders are always fighting the feelings and asking themselves, *"am I really the leader my team thinks I am?"* This way of thinking is called imposter syndrome. It is like a disease that will cloud the judgments of a leader. Leaving them with a wave of self-doubt.

Knowing your leadership rides on your self-confidence makes it an essential part of the way you lead. You must change the question asked earlier and said, *"I am good enough, and I am the leader my teams says I am."*

Overcoming Fear: We all have fears. It may even be hard to put your worries aside to complete a task. You may have a fear of speaking, a fear of loss, or a fear of making a mistake. All of these are fears that people really do have. When you have these fears, the biggest questions that come to mind are all "what if" questions. Fears are a part of who we are. If you say you have no concern, you are not being honest with yourself.

Leaders are not exempt from having fears. You must start by recognizing your worries. Now that you know what your worries are, take charge and handle it effectively that will allow you to continue with your leadership roles.

Following Through: Have you ever felt like you do not have enough time to do everything? Things always happen, such as life. You are probably still as busy as a leader. I know I am! You are being pulled in all sorts of directions, such as emergencies, distractions, and opportunities that come up. There is no wonder why you are so busy. These all create issues of not following through with tasks that need to be done. Think about it, about 90% of your plans probably do not meet the excepted requirements. We could say they fall short.

The trick is the organization. I use to think my friends in school were crazy because they keep such a tight schedule. Now that I am a leader, I can see why it is so important. Having a plan helps you follow through with all your tasks and things that need to be finished. If you cannot complete them during the scheduled time, schedule a time where they get finished. The trick is to follow your schedule, as well.

Stress and Anxiety: Being a leader can be stressful. It could also cause a great deal of anxiety. With all the pressures of leadership,this can be considered normal. You are already facing many challenges. Those challenges may create another challenge of stress and anxiety. Keep in mind, if it gets to be more than you can handle, it could cause you to have a hard time making the right choices and leading your team.

It is so essential for you to have control over your stress and anxiety. Do not let it control you. During my time as a leader in the military, I would get bad headaches. These headaches made it impossible for me to fulfill my duties as a leader. I went through several tests and a CAT scan. They all came back negative. I eventually realized it was the stress and anxiety that I was experiencing. At that time, I changed my leadership style to work better for me to cope. I still get them but not as bad or as often. This is due to learning to cope with stress and anxiety.

Staying Motivated: You have probably had a bad day that you do not want to relive. It was so bad that all you wanted to do was go home and not think about it. The problem is it is only lunchtime. What caused it to be so bad? Do not worry. We have all had those types of days. When you get home, all you do is think about the day.

It is hard to stay motivated when the day's events do not give you a reason to be motivated. The best solution is to think about your team and why you become a leader. That alone gives you a senseof your motivation. Your team needs a leader. They need that motivation. If you are not motivated, they are not motivated.

Avoid the Burnout: Look at all those challenges we have already read about. Are you burned out yet? It is easy to feel burnout. Being a leader is challenging. Some leaders push themselves to the point of exhaustion. You never see the rest, and they work hours that are insane.

When you feel burnout, who are you helping? You cannot think straight. You cannot be an effective leader. It is essential to take time for yourself. When I look at all the jobs I have had, I hardly never take a vacation. Others may wonder why I would not feel burnout. The answer is simple, *"I leave work at the office and enjoy my time away."* I do not bring work home. It is essential to keep them separate.

Vulnerability: Vulnerability is like humility. It is just as important. For a prideful leader, it is complicated to admit when they are wrong. They cannot learn from their mistakes. They could not be exceptional leaders until they tackle this obstacle. It is like wrapping all the challenges I have mention thus far into one. It does not show weakness, as some leaders may think. In fact, it is just the opposite. It shows strength in your leadership ability to lead your team.

Skill Challenges: The Ability Tests

Internal challenges are not the only challenges that you may see. You will face challenges that test your skills. In a way, all these challenges work together. Your internal challenges will affect your decisions for every obstacle you face.

That is not to say you cannot handle them. Every skill can be perfected. You can also learn new skills that you have not discovered yet. Think about every challenge you face as a leader in a way to grow. They are fundamental for growth and strength as a leader. Learn from them and better your leadership skills. Be doing this, you will elevate you and your team to new heights.

Continue to keepyour team motivated and inspired: You have worked on self-motivation. This is a valuable trait you must have as a leader. However, that is not all. A leader must provide the same for their team. This can be just as challenging.

Expect that every team member will question the decisions you make. They may or may not voice their opinion. Yet, the thoughts are still there. Your team wants a reason to be at work. They need an understanding of what is going on. It is your job to help them stay focused. Inspire them! Give them a goal to achieve. Make it fun and help develop them to be an exceptional leader. Set the example and show them the way.

When your team feels the burnout, create a way to inspire them. Perhaps add incentives to motivate them to do better. Give them breaks to rest from what they are doing.

Couching, developing, and mentoring your team: Your team is not working just because they need a job. Chances are they are thinking about their careers. They want to know what it takes to grow and become successful. It is your job to make it happen. How do you do that? Simple, push them, given them tasks they can learn from, and direct them.

Do not think of it as being their boss. Think of it as you are their mentor. It is your job to see what they can and cannot do. Find their strengths and weaknesses. Challenge their weaknesses. Find ways they can turn them into strengths.

Create a high standard. Guide and support your team. Lead and show your team the way to meet this standard. Watch them exceed it and shoot higher. Take the time to recognize their hard work. Reward them and let them know they matter.

Managing resources and your team: Many leaders think that micromanaging and managing are the same things. The truth is they are not. They are far from the same. Micromanaging is when you are always looking for your team's shoulders and telling them everything they need to do and the way to do it.

Do not become a micromanager. You should be a problem-solver. Let your team handle the tasks independently. They are good at what they can do. Let them do it so they can grow from the experience.

Do not think you can delegate the work to just anyone. It is not about just giving it to someone to do the job because you do not want to handle it. It is about letting your team do the job they were hired to do. It is about giving your team members the power to grow from the experience.

Your own skill development: As a leader, it is essential to develop your team. However, leaders tend to forget about themselves. You always want to build and grow your leadership skills. Yes, your team is essential. You are their leader and are just as important. An exceptional leader is always finding ways to enhance their skills.

We talk about burnout, and this personal development will help you with burnout to be a more proactive and effective leader. Basically, it comes down to taking care of yourself.

Guiding changes: You have heard the saying, *"the only thing that is constant is change."* Today that is a famous saying. Especially in a world that is always changing. It is something we can count on to stay consistent. Many decades ago, the expression was part of profound philosophy in the world.

What does that mean for you? Simple, you must be equipped to take on those changes. For example, look at doctors. There is always a new medication or procedure that is coming out. A doctor must continuously be learning new things to stay caught up with these changes. Usually, once you have learned about this recent change, you must know about another one. It never ends. That is what keeps life exciting.

Sometimes you can predict change. Look at our example of the doctor. They already know that something new will be out by the time they learn about the current one. However, change is usually unpredictable. That is why it is essential to be prepared for anything life throughs at you and be in a constant state of learning.

Making hard decisions: It is sad when I come across a leader who is always looking for the easy way out. Thrust me, there is one. The unfortunate thing is it will always be the wrong choice. You will still be faced with hard decisions. Some are easier than others—however, the easy, what out is never the right solution.

It can be hard to make decisions that will affect the team. You have their careers in your hands. Keep this in mind, every decision you make will be yours to live with. I always ask myself, *"what will be the consequences of my decision?"* Every choice you make will always have a consequence. It could be good or bad consequences, yet they are there.

Do not be afraid of the decision was the wrong one. You are not perfect. It is going to happen. The point is, you still need to make a decision. Take the bad ones as a learning experience for the next time you are faced with the same issue.

An exceptional leader will make decisions, no matter how hard they may be. Yet, they still will not lose any sleep over the choices they make regardless if it had a good or bad outcome. They know they made the right call and can learn from the harmful results.

Communication Challenges: Those that Threaten Your Team Dynamics

There are so many challenges you will face as a leader. You have challenges with yourself and ones that attack your abilities. However, one that I consider may be the biggest challenge is communication. For example, it is like someone talking to you in Chinese, and you know English. So much can be lost in translation. When there are gaps, people tend to find substitutes for those gaps.

Having everyone on the same page: Everyone in your team or organization is different. You will not find two identical people. With all the different ways of life, it is hard to get everyone on the same page. This can prove to be very challenging.

The best way to battle this challenge is to understand the people on your team. Learn about them and approach them in a way that works best for them. Sometimes you may need to present it in several different forms to ensure everyone is on the same page.

Dealing with issues and conflicts: Conflicts and problems arise when working closely together, such as your team. That is life. It happens. There are so many situations that could cause them to get worse.

Remember, there is always a solution. Start by understanding that you cannot avoid issues coming up or conflicts happening. Tough decisions may need to be made to resolve the issue. To strengthen your team, you need to make those tough choices of resolutions. Once the problems are solved, productivity will rise again.

Giving bad news: Nobody likes bad news. Most importantly, nobody wants to deliver bad news. This is one of the hardest things to do. In the military during a deployment, the worse thing a commander dreads taking that long road to a soldier home to give the bad news of their child not coming home for dinner. Granted, you will never need to provide that type of bad news.

Giving any kind of bad news to any leader will make you feel like the military commander. You dread it. Mistakes happen. Things may never go as you originally planned. You may even be labeled as *"the bad guy."* Yet, the issue must be addressed.

One of the biggest things to remember is empathy. You can deliver bad news but connect with the team member is essential. Ensure they understand the situation clearly yet sympathize with them and help them through the process. They need to know you are there for them, and you care as their leader.

Crisis Challenges: Those Found in a Crisis

One of the biggest challenges for a leader is facing the unexpected. The basics are natural disasters or the upheaval economy. Some others are catastrophic, a product that fails to launch, or a global pandemic. You cannot plan for these things happening. The only thing you can do is prepare yourself for the unexpected.

For example, where I grew up, we lived on a fault line for earthquakes. The mountains protected us for the most part. I cannot control the weather or what the earth is going to do. To fight this natural disaster, the schools regularly perform earthquake drills and educate the student about earthquakes. You can prepare for them even when you cannot prevent them.

Stay positive even in the most challenging situations: One of the hardest things to do is stay positive in every case. This is due to how it is easier to be negative in most situations. Trust me, it takes practice to be positive in all conditions. We have emotions, and sometimes they take over. When there is a bad situation or bad news needs to be given, the most challenging thing can be positive.

Having a positive outlook even in the most diverse situations. It shows who you are as a leader. It can show your team that it is ok to make mistakes. There is always a reason to be optimistic.

When a ship is traveling the seas, they look at a lighthouse to be a beacon of light to help them navigate at night when close to land. It is the same for your team. They look at you as their leader as that same beacon for guidance. This becomes more so in circumstances that appear more complicated.

Betransparent and honest at all times: You may feel the best way to protect your team from the issues is to sugarcoat them. You do not want to hurt them or make them worry. When they are hurt or worried, then productivity goes down. You can learn about your team. However, is this the best way?

Hiding things from the team that may affect them is a bad idea. Transparency is important. They can take it. Chances are they already know, and they can see right through you. I will maintain the respect from them if you keep it real. You worked hard for them to respect you. If you start sugarcoating it, that respects slowly vanish.

Projecting your calmness: When it is human nature to have a fight-or-flight response, being calm is very difficult to achieve. How can you cast your peace onto the team if you cannot stay calm yourself? As a leader, you need to learn to remain calm in every situation. It takes practice.

When the situation gets worse, it is hard to stay calm. Although this is when your team needs to see you calm more than anything. It helps your team feel more secured about the situation. They start feeling they can get through the bad together. There is great power in staying calm. It is contagious. If your team sees you are relaxed, they will not worry about the bad as much.

You are not a robot, keep it human: Your team must see that you are also human. That means you make mistakes and are not perfect. They need to know who you are. You have a family, emotions, and a life outside of work. You set the example for your team. Show them you do not run like a machine.

How to Overcome Your Leadership Challenges

With all these challenges you face, you may still have the question, *"how do you overcome them?"* The best answer is you. That is right. You are the only one with the power to overcome all these challenges and become an excellent leader.

Create your decision frame: It takes practice to overcome challenges. It will not happen overnight. Practice making decisions. Have a plan for how you are going to tackle every situation and challenge you may face. The better decision-maker you become, the easier it is to overcome challenges.

A great place to start is to understand your personal beliefs and attitudes. Break them down into a clear picture. Use this to measure your decision-making skills.

Sometimes, it is hard to get started. Maybe you do not know where to start. You need a framework that will help focus on what is important to you as a person. Here are some necessary steps to get you started.

1. **Clear purpose:** What makes you a good leader? Why do you exist in the company or your team? Search hard inside you for these answers. Once you have them, hold tight to what you find.
2. **Vision clarification:** Look at your team. Do they understand what it is like to have a win? If not, find out yourself what a win likes like on your team and share it with your team. Help them see what it is like to always be on a winning team.
3. **Values defined:** What are the values that are the most important to you and are nonnegotiable? We all have values that we hold dear to us. Those values are what makes us a great leader.

4. **Lights, Camera, Action:** Take all the information about your vision, values, and purpose into consideration. These will help you to become a better decision-maker and leader.

It does not seem hard. There are only four steps. The best part is how they all come from deep inside you. This is only an example to get you started. With a useful framework, you will find every decision more comfortablewith making and will often be the correct decision. You will become a proactive leader instead of a reactive leader.

Stop being a leader of fear: Everyone feels fear. It is natural and normal. It is not unhealthy to feel fear. It becomes harmful if it takes over your decision-making. Some leaders think that the opposite of fear would be courage. To be honest, being courageous does not mean you do not have a feeling of anxiety. It just means you face fear head-on and act.

It is impossible to not be fearful. However, it is the actions you take in the face of those fears. When you allow your fears to control your actions, lousy decision-making starts to happen. It is ok to feel fear but do not let that fear take over your ability to lead.

Look at the great leaders in history, do they feel fear? Yes, they do. That is what makes them so great. They learned to tackle their concerns and let them work for them instead of against them. Use your framework and include your fears. Acknowledge them and know how to take them head-on.

Your efforts must be prioritized: Life as a leader can get hectic. Your life may be wild. You have the plan and have put it into play. Yet, it still seems like it is not enough. It may not be. Get organized and set priorities.

There is a concept I want you to remember. It is called the Pareto Principle. You may also know it as the 80/20 rule. Think about the two numbers a percent. The best way to break it down is that 80% of your impact as a lead will only come from 20% of your action or the things you decide. That means, most of the outcomes are from only 20% of your doings. Therefore, you need to prioritize that 20% and put it at the top.

I want you to stop and think about all the things you need to be done. Lay it all out on the table. This may take a while or be a very long list. If you cannot go it now, mark this page and come back to it. This is important to help you become an exceptional leader.

Now that you have a list set a rank of priority from 1 – 10. This makes 1 having the highest priority, and 10 will be the lowest priority. If you are at a computer, you can make your list with excel. That way, once you have them ranked, you can do a sort automatically. If you are not at the computer, I would suggest transferring it to excel when you can.

Going back to the Pareto Principle, if your list has a 1 or 2, it affects most of your impact. All your 3s to 7s are maybe worthwhile. If you have any 8s to 10s, they most likely will not impact your team at all. Your 1s and 2s are where changes happen. Those are the items that will make the most significant impact on your decisions and your team.

Go back to your list. Sort it by the number and highlight each group. I would use red for the 1s and 2s. I would use yellow for the 3s to 7s, and for the 8s to 10s, I would use green. It should look like a stoplight. This would help you remember what each color means. Red would mean top priority, yellow would mean cautious or notessential, and green would suggest it is ok to let it go or not get to it right away.

You are probably reading through this and wondering, *"what is the point of doing this?"* If you do not do it and stay organized on the most important and impact the team the most, you may spend more time on the less impactful things. It is like freezing time. Your team will stop moving forward or will be moving slower than a tortoise. Through this principle, you will see your team moving forward and set them up for success.

Design a psychologically safe atmosphere: Your team wants to feel safe when they come to work. You owe it to your team. There is a saying, *"the best work happens in a safe environment."* It is true. When your team feels safe to be at work and talk to you about anything, the communication line is open, and the productivity is skyrocketed.

The Best Work Happens in a Safe Environment.

It is not easy to create a psychologically, safe workplace. It takes hard work and commitment to make it happen. It is not only the responsibility of the leader. It takes the team to create this type of environment. To make this happen, it requires two significant factors. It needs honesty among you and your team and complete transparency. This will create an atmosphere of trust.

You may not know where to begin. Let me give you a secret: listen to your team. Perfect the art of listening. Your teams want to feel they are heard. You cannot listen to them if you do not listen. This does not mean sitting there and letting them talk. It means fully understanding and knowing what they are saying. Listen to what they say and be able to recall the conversation if needed. I usually take notes afterward to keep in their file. That way, you can reference them later if needed. Do not be afraid to write things down during the conversation. It shows that you really care. Especially if it is concerning issues that must be addressed.

You would be surprised by the difference it makes on your team when they feel their leader is listening to them. Leadership requires trust. Everything we have suggested throughout this chapter and book will help to build trust within your team. Your team will become more productive and will not want to let you down just as you heard them and have not let them down.

When everyone is on the same page and has the same goals, it will elevate you and your team to the next level or two. It is better and more exciting when you know you are not alone. You may be the leader, but it takes the team to make things happen.

Have a mindset that is always growing: They say leaders are learners. This is only partly true. Leaders are still learning. However, they are also educators, mentors, and friends, just to name a few. A leader has so many responsibilities and hats to wear. Your mindset should always be one of growth. That does not mean you only focus on your own personal development. It also means that you help the growth of your team.

I also think of it this way, *"I want my team members to one day to become my leader."* This is the same aspect as the train the trainer. You are training future leaders. One day they will be where you are or further. What things can you do now that will affect your team's growth and progression in the future? Simon Sinek said, *"Leadership is a choice. It is not a rank."* Take on the challenges of full force and be an exceptional leader.

Chapter 12: Techniques for Overcoming Issues

The ability to shift into different roles between being an effective team leader to being whatever role a person can become is the most significant skill a leader should master. However, switching into this role does not come naturally and might take years to perfect. The act itself is likely to raise a concept of potential doubt to the leader and create management mishaps in the long run. Selecting a roleyou may not be suited tobe a requirement set by the company or the team members' attitudes. If the action is not managed correctly, it will pave a way to more leadership issues.

Here are ways a leader can avoid and overcome these leadership issues.

> ➢ Breaks are necessary to become productive by preserving energy and recharging a mental health state.
> ➢ Apply the "do not bring your work home" practice. Make their home a safe place from your work.
> ➢ Ask for help when needed. It is neither ignorance nor prideful to ask for help.
> ➢ When pressure arises during a workday, refresh by taking a short walk outside the office, do some meditation, or consider exercising.
> ➢ Strengthen their communication and relationship with your team.

To avoid these issuesfrom happening, leaders can practice self-awareness and prevent the harmful effects of leadership. Somehow a portion of these issues are bound in nature and cannot be controlled, yet how they respond to these issues is manageable.

Charismatic Leadership

This type of leader's audience is usually driven by the charm and compelling attractiveness of the person. They use joy, confidence, sense of style, and physical appearance to influence people to follow them. Hence,the root word *"charisma"* comes from.

They are sometimes called *"transformational leaders"*to lead with firm conviction and maintain an immense difference. Dr. Martin Luther King, Jr is an excellent example of a charismatic leader who used powerful words in his speech to persuade an audience to make a positive change in the lives of millions.

Charismatic leaders are fluent in verbal communication and articulation. They know how to create a deep connection to their audience on a deeper level and giving a sense of emotion. This is usually beneficial for a person trying to run for office. They are perceived as leaders who know what they want and how to achieve it, making them the person fit for the job to create a greater good in society.

Benefits of Charismatic Leadership

Every public and private sector needs at least one charismatic leader to represent their business. An in-depth, motivated, and the great speaker will lead people to follow them. For instance, in a government setting, a charismatic leader will run for office and likely succeed in gathering voters due to excellent physical appearance and communication delivery, which drives people to come after them. An effective leader of a country needs to be a person of conviction, who knows how to stand up with other people who have an opposite view. In this ever-changing world at a swift pace, a country's leaders should at least be proper and robust. The world needs more of them.

Charismatic leaders are known to be people with conviction because they fight for what they know is right and seems right. They are willing to stand up to prove their conviction to the people with a different state of view, most especially in the way they are leading. They motivate their people to become better leaders themselves. They are famous for their courage. They show to create a quality and a better life for the people they are leading.

Charismatic leaders are motivated and easily influence others to follow them. They thrive for change and are committed to delivering their vision into factual realities. They create a vision and a common goal for their followers to grasp clearly and readily understood. Hence, they complete tasks with confidence that it will bring positive results.

- ➢ Advantages of Charismatic Leadership
    - ○ Through a charismatic leader's influence, they bring people together to work with the same vision and purpose.
    - ○ They increase the loyalty and commitment of the team to perform better.
    - ○ A charismatic leader focuses on growth and improvement than using punishment as a learning solution.
    - ○ They bring different groups of people, such as organizations, societies, and people, to become committed to the primary goal.
    - ○ The leader reiterates the importance of learning from their own mistakes, to become better individuals.
    - ○ They lead a team of people with a more excellent vision and an effective strategy.

- ➢ Disadvantages of Charismatic Leadership

- Leaders may put too much focus on their good deeds that they become arrogant.
- Subordinates may become too dependent on the leader and may suffer without their presence.
- These leaders may overlook their mistakes with their good deeds and not learn from them.
- Due to the influence the position carries, charismatic leaders may feel they are above the law and may not be reprimanded when things have gone wrong.

The Needs of a Charismatic Leader to Be Successful

It may seem that a charismatic leader may have all the qualities a leader should have, yet they still need to have other things that can help them become even more successful. Being admirable is just one of the many tools a leader must possess.

To be consistently successful, charismatic leaders need to have a vision and a talented team of skilled individuals. For instance, at least a member of a unit should be great in public relations. They are in charge of the leader's available image, media, press that shapes the leader's public opinion, and the business they represent. Together they will lead a business or a company's various life stages to success. This team should be composed of discrete people with talents that can make their goals a reality. A leader without a successful team cannot properly function well. The leader is only as good as their team. With no crew, a leader is irrelevant.

A charismatic leader must also have ethics and commitment to practical knowledge. They must always remember their purpose of being a leader to serve and lead, not immorally, or abuse power. They also need to have integrity, having the conviction of doing the right thing even when nobody is looking without the need forrecognition. They need to be selfless and have a more significant concern for the people they lead. They must understand their aspirations and listen to their voices. They must be willing to sacrifice and risk essential things to create change and make a difference in their lives. After all, leadership is about serving people, no matter what style and type a leader may have.Leaders who understand the severity of their vision and purpose can become efficient and compassionate leaders.

All these are important for you to maintaingood governance and leadership. What is more essential is that a leader and their people should work for everyone's goodness. This way, the world would become a better place one action at a time.

Chapter 13: Essential Keys for Uncertainty

Leadership can be a challenge, regardless of the circumstances. In good or bad times, there will always be a challenge for even the best leaders. You are attempting to balance your needs and your team's needs. You also are thinking about their future.Some factors come into play, such as the individual personalities of your team. Think about the communication that is involved. You have to know how to communicate with people across all playing fields. Let us not forget about all the unexpected issues that may arise with all these uncertainties. The list can go on for miles. You must be prepared for everything.

Many of the leader leaders are stuck in their own ways. They feel, why to reinvent the wheel if it already works. The problem with the practice of think ng in leadership is the way our future is becoming more advanced. That means our old ways are history. What may have worked then does not work now. Which brings us back to what I have said many times, leaders are always learning. It is your job to keep up with the times. As times change, your leadership style will change.

An exceptional leader will make those changes and continue to learn with the same strong leadership they are known for. You should adapt to the times cf now and no longer live in the past. These changes bring new and exciting problems that will make you think. However, they will also make you a better leader.

Utilize these changes and let them work for you. Advance your leadership and continue to be an exceptional leader. It does not matter the uncertainty; you will know how to handle them and continue to lead your team while conforming to the future in leadership. There is a trick to preparing yourself for the unexpected.

For You to Serve Others, Look at Your Own Needs

This seems like the easiest thing to do. You may find that you are not going as good of a job as you think. This is a crucial part of being an exceptional leader and knowing what to do during crunch time.

Think about it, if you fall apart during a task, what will happen to the team? The will ultimately see failure. They cannot succeed if you cannot hold your own as a leader. The uncertainty will require a lot of energy when leading. It is like walking into an unknown part of the woods. You know the woods like the back of your hand; however, you do not know this part at all. Every day you must be at your best. Here are a few ways to take care of your own needs so that you can take care of your team.

> ➢ The first place to start is the most obvious. Make sure you are taking outstanding care of yourself physically. This means shower, brush teeth,

meditate, exercise, and so on. You might wonder why I said meditate in this area. The reason will lead to the next point. However, it also helps you to stay focused.

➤ You will want to create a personal space. This is a way to recharge yourself and clear your head to make better judgments as a leader. There are a variety of things you can do. A great way to clear your mind is through meditation. However, you can also read books or material not related to work or listen to music. The biggest thing is to take your mind off of work so that you can get a short break.

➤ It does not matter if you are a new leader or have been a leader for centuries; you need a support channel. This is where you find support from your peers, family, friends, and so on. Your support can come from anyone. If you noticed, it could be from outside or within your organization. This support will help you to stop jumping into action first. You must slow down and think about what you are doing and how to attack each issue. Make a plan before acting on the subject.

Communication is Essential

In the military, change comes at the last minute, and you must adjust to the changes. They should come as the task is being performed or a few days in advance. Either way, communication is essential for your team to understand what is being asked of them.

One of the most effective tools is communication. It does take practice to perfect it within your leadership. You will want to be clear about what is needed. Your entire team needs to be on the same page. Always be prepared for change and know how to communicate those changes. Here are a few things to consider on your path to improve your communication in leadership.

➤ For starters, do not think you have all the answers. Therefore, do not wait until you do have all the answers. If you pretend you have all the answers, your team will see right through you, and you will start to lose their trust in you as a leader.

➤ When there is information that is given, you want to ensure you have clarity. Make sure you know what is being asked of you and your team. Ask questions! The way this is done is through communication. Consistently review, reinforce, reiterate, and reassure your team. They need that from you. This takes a great deal of communication and exceptional leadership.

➤ Keep in mind, communication is a never-ending process. Email, meetings, evaluations, and so on are all types of communication. An exceptional leader knows how to use each type. Anything that is sent or receiving information is communication.

- ➤ There will be times where it may seem to be overwhelming by the unknown. It way affects your own way of communication. There is a trick to help you deal with this. Ask yourself the following questions:
    - ○ What do we know? This can be as easy as saying, this is a mess and the organization is always changing. The main thing is that validation.
    - ○ What is it we do not know?
    - ○ What are we able to do?
    - ○ When will you or your team hear from the leadership again?

Think About the Shared Goals and Focus on Them

Every leader has anxiety, worry, or distractions that cause a challenge in their leadership. These are even greater when there is a lot of uncertainty. Some, such as I, also have headaches that creates a significant challenge in the way you lead. Regardless of all these challenges, keep focused. You need to show your team that it is essential to stay focused on your shared goals. Give them stability and sight to see the path as they move forward. Here are a few ideas that will help with your focus through this ever-changing world.

- ➤ As you get a task and communicate it to your team, you will want to collaborate on how to perform this task the most effectively. Do this early in the project. Do not wait until the last minute, and then you would feel you must rush the job and not meet the attended standards. You will also want to meet with your team throughout the project and help them stay focused. There are strengths in numbers. This is even true for your team. You can accomplish more as a team than you can as individuals.
- ➤ One of the most important things to remember, create a safe environment for your team. They need to feel that security can say anything has complete participation and contribute to the project and team.

Find a Way to Connect with Your Team

Every leader wants a healthy team. The most successful teams and leaders are those with that healthy team. More so, a group that is connected. This plays an essential part in facing adversity together. Be creative and think outside the box. Here are a few other ideas of keeping a healthy connection within your team.

- ➤ Have regular meetings with your team. Ensure you talk about the key points and allow each member to contribute to the discussion. It does not matter what type of meeting it is. It can even be a non-traditional method, such as virtual. The point has those meetings as a team regularly.

> Try a slightly different approach. You can consider a virtual happy hour within your team. This is a way to bring up morale and allow the flow of communication within your team. It can be as simple as a check-in virtually, having a poll set for your team to answer questions, or having a full conversation through a team chat board to share thoughts and issues.
> One of my favorites is team building activities. These demonstrate trust and cohesion among your team. You can do trust falls, building things out of different objects, and so on. Make it fun and teach your team to work together to solve problems and trust each other within the group.
> Do not think you are the only one with ideas. Let your team share their thoughts. You may be surprised by what they come up with. This also gives them a sense of having a say in their leadership development. They may have ideas you never thought of.

Your Expectations are Negotiable

I want you to put yourself seated at a magic show. Do you know what the magician will do? Of course, you do. Why? Because they said, they will do it. It is an illusion that was already created and practiced for many years before coming to the stage.

Now, let us look at real like. Is life predictable? Of course not. Life is the most unpredictable adventure you will take. With life being so unpredictable, you must be flexible and willing to look at situations from all sides. Do not get stuck thinking, *"that is the way it has always been done."* If you feel this way, you have already failed.

You will always be adjusting and re-evaluating your expectations to fit inline with the changing organization and world. Find ways to take advantage of what you have now. Then prepare for what the future may hold and adjust as needed.

> Look closely at your work. Better yet, imagine using a scope to get a real close look. What do you see? What changes can be made? This is the best way to think about it. You should focus on the areas that need the most attention and is more viable. If you are in sales, you may focus on the changes that have been made to sales. How did they affect your current sales and opportunities?
> You may want to think about finding new ways with your partnerships and clients to create methods that can support everyone in the organization or your team.
> Sometimes, you have ideas that you put on the backburner. Perhaps, they did not fit into your situation at that time. However, what about how?

Revisit those ideas. Not all solutionsworkin every case. Although the old ideas may fit the current situation.

> There is a saying, *"time is money."* Your time is valuable even when you have downtime. This is a great time for team training and personal development. Find areas that you and your team need to work on. Create a training environment and learn together. You may want to try a *"train the trainer"* type of program within your team or organization. This is where you have trained your team. Now it is time to put them to the test and allow them to conduct the next training. You could give them a topic or area if you want. To test their leadership skills, you can even let them decide on the subject within the spectrum of their job or position.

You need much more than the ability to deal with the challenges when facing uncertainty. You must know how to look into the future and anticipate what it holds for you and your team. Having the right strategies is very important. Always have a plan. Evaluate your position and team. Find areas that in improving and plan.

You will eventually be like a psychic for your team. You will look into your crystal ball and see what will happen based on your decisions. The new normal will be created by the choices you make as the future is not written, and the world is always changing. Focus on your strengths and skills. Use them to face the uncertainty head-on. Take your team into a successful future and be the exceptional leader they deserve.

Chapter 14: Charismatic Leadership and the Affects on the Team

A Charismatic Leader has several traits that allow them to be exceptional leaders. Is that not the goal we all are trying to achieve? The best of the best will have many of these attributes, if not all of them.

Communication

These types of leaders are fluent in communication. They have extraordinary skills when speaking to people, which aids in creating a difference, influence the target audience, and motivates people. This is best for leaders who have a team of demotivated people, for instance, a coach who is about to lose a game, a president whose country is experiencing a catastrophe, or maybe a supervisor with a failed project. Through their charisma and exceptional usage of words, they can turn a sour moment into a second opportunity for them to get better.

Maturity

The balance between the demand for quick solutions to modern business problems and the maturity that needs to reflect with those solutions are precarious. Developing maturity and wisdom takes years to master.A charismatic leader must display maturity and character in every decision they make. He must be matured enough to draw from the experience to create effective resolutions.

A mature leader has patience, values work relationships, shows empathy towards others, and knows how to avoid conflicts. They know how to differentiate personal from business affairs and make sure that they are never in dispute.

Humility

Every so often, when a person reaches a significantly high disposition in life, they become proud. They put too much value on external appearance, accomplishments, and self-confidence that they began losing humility.

Charismatic leaders need to have a sense of humility. They should know how to empathize with their employees and extend a helping hand when it is required.They should add value to their member's skills and help them produce impactful contributions to the company.

A charismatic leader knows how to accept their own weaknesses and failures. They need to be able to point out their limitations and are not afraid of them. They also take responsibility for their wrong actions and correct them for future use. They have a humble perspective by being open to criticism and always aiming for continuous growth.

Compassion
Having a pleasant personality and desirable physical appearance is not enough to become an effective leader. A charismatic leader knows how to balance appearance and their actions. They seek to create influence and serve people with passion. They are serious about creating a difference in their team's lives and aims to make a difference during their time of the ruling.

They show compassion through sharing their knowledge, resources, talents, insights, and anything more useful for helping others without asking too much in return.

Substance
A leader of substance is usually distinguished as a person who is at their most effective. Charismatic leaders *"walk the talk"* instead of capturing attention only through a façade. Leaders of substance create an impact on people and know-how to deliver their words through actions.

They value the trust of their people by meeting the promises made to them. They make a commitment to turn the hopes of their team into something more valuable and real. A charismatic leader with substance has a word of honor.

Confidence
A leader's self-confidence stems from not just from being attractive but rather from being optimistic in his decisions. They think positively about the future of their leadership, their team, and commit to taking any possible way to achieve their goals. They are also willing to take a risk if necessary, to turn aspirations into reality.

A self-confident leader knows how to handle things without practicing self-doubts. They focus on their competence, capabilities, most vital talents, and strengths. They use these self-features to the benefit of the team and the people who trust them.

Positive Body Language
Everything about a charismatic leader shows positivism, most especially in their body language. They create a strong connection with gestures such as making eye contact with the person they are talking to; they smile and maintain a relaxed and open facial expression. Authenticity is also important; people can sense a

fake leader once they see one. A leader should be charismatic by showing who they really are.

Listening Skills

A good leader is also a good listener. There is nothing more effective than a person who hears the voices of their team. A charismatic leader who is good in words must also be better in active listening. They pay attention to what their team is saying and sending appropriate help when needed.Leaders who know how to listen create trustworthy relationships with their subordinates.

Self-Monitoring

To create a persona of a good leader, one must practice self-monitoring or self-awareness. They must become aware of their personality, how people perceivetheir image and their words. They must accept the fact that they will continuously watch them. Thus, it is always essential for a leader to portray theright image of themselves.

Self-Improvement

Since leaders are not born but rather made, leadership thrives for continuous learning and growth. A charismatic leader has self-improvement with a constant pursuit of making themself better in every aspect of their life. They acknowledge their own qualities from other leaders, conceding them as their own better features,makingthem charismatic.

Characteristics distinguish an attribute of a person, while qualities are characteristics for being a good and purposely well fit person for the job. It is the characteristic of a person who creates a pleasant image, yet their qualities make them a charismatic leader. It is their qualities that put substance into their role as a leader.

They Earn Respect

People tend to follow a leader that they can count on to help them achieve the essential things. They prefer a leader who earns their trust by keeping their words and turning them words into actions. A leader who deserves the respect of their team shows respect in everything he does. They put a commitment to their work and practice servant leadership.

They Have the Halo Effect

A famous saying states,*"Attractive people are perceived to be smarter, funnier, and more likable than less attractive ones."*It shows that the physical image of a person can be perceived as their character.

The halo effect is a perception of a person's single trait, which ultimately makes up the person's character's overall impression. This is best for companies who have a good reputation in doing a business, which also creates an image of having better leaders.

Develop Acceptance

Charismatic leaders know how to accept both their good and bad traits. They develop charisma by working on themselves first. Good leaders will maintain self-acceptance by practicing self-awareness. They are aware of their strengths and weaknesses while working their way out of these qualities and becominginfluential leaders.

Responsible

Responsible leadership is all about taking ownership of the outcomes they produce, continuous self-development, and others' treatment. A responsible leader is tasked to handle problems dispensed by the company or organization they represent. They develop strategies to address those problems and commit a constant delivery of positive results.

Result Driven

One of the good qualities of a charismatic leader is they are result-driven. They put immense focus on achieving the results they were tasked to accomplish. A charismatic leader creates strategies and critical set-up processes that aim to deliver better results. They are willing to look for solutions in any possible way that will help them make a decision.

They create a vision that indicates a better picture of the results they wanted to achieve. They then determine the factors and process of attaining them, continuing to direct the right process until they produce the desired results.

These are only a small handful of all the characteristics a charismatic leader will have. Take the time to find what works for you and continue your learning path and become a charismatic leader. It is up to you to find that exceptional leader inside you.

Chapter 15: Modeling Positive Leadership Behavior

A leader is a model for everyone around them. It does not matter if you have bad, exemplary, or exceptional leadership. You set the example for everyone else. Do not think of the behavior itself. Instead, think of the value your behavior has on the team.

For example, you are always letting your team know how important it is to work as a team; yet you do not spend time working with your team as the leader. How do you think your squad feels? It is essential to practice what you tell them to do. To avoid this, you should consider a few extra tips.

Model Personal Values

Every leader has personal values that govern their actions. They work hard to maintain those values. Exceptional leaders will stay try to what they believe. This must show through by the way the act.

For example, you promote having acceptable language in the work environment. You would not let your team go around cussing when you know it is against your values. It is like this with all your valuables. As a leader, you set the example. You show others the way should act and behave.

Encouraging Self-Determination

An exceptional leader encourages their team to stand on their own and think for themselves. The best way of doing this is by showing them how. This does not mean you take their hand and work them through it. It means to continue to set the example so they can see how it is done. It is like playing follow the leader. You set the benchmark for them to follow.

Encourage Positivity

Having a positive workplace is essential to having a great team. Through positivity in the group, you will see positive interaction among your team. This will increase productivity.

Set High Expectations

Many leaders like to set high expectations that seem unobtainable. This is one of the biggest mistakes a leader can make. You are setting your team up for failure. Evaluate your expectations and set them high. However, make sure you can reach them. When you set high expectations, you are committing to them as well as your team. Make sure you live up to them and deliver on those expectations.

Value Your Team

Give value to your team. Without your team, you can not be the leader you want to be. They are the ones who make you an exceptional leader. Consistently give them value by showing them you listen and are a part of the team. Not just the leader. Do your part and take their opinions to heart. They want to feel like they have been heard.

When issues happen within the team and between team members, get them resolves as soon as possible. Keep that cohesion you have developed and maintain a strong team that knows how to work together to make things happen.

As a leader, you want your team to know you are there for them. They need to understand they will always have your support, willingness to help them when needed, and you want to help them develop their skills. Be open about it.

Proper Feedback

Giving feedback is just as essential as the other areas. It is human nature to give negative feedback. It seems like it is easy to tell others what they are doing wrong. Try it for one week with your team. Go all week, and the only kind of feedback you give them is harmful. Wait! Before doing this, think about how they may feel. Better yet, put yourself in their shoes and ask yourself how it would make you think. With that said, you may be thinking twice before wanting to give negative feedback to your team. You will find that if all your team ever hears is what they are doing wrong, your productivity will be extremely low. They will not want to work with someone who is always negative. There will be times where negative feedback is necessary. However, there is a way to give it tonot lose respect and maintain a positive environment.

Giving feedback is like making a sandwich. You want to always focus on the future. Start with positive feedback. Let them know how much you appreciate them. Keep in mind, every negative thing should be complemented by two positive things. Even with the negative, help them understand it is for them to grow and become great leaders themselves. Always focus mostly on the positive.

Being Influential

Being a leader is not about holding a title. A former British prime minister, Margaret Thatcher, said it best when she said, *"Being in power is like being a lady. If you have to tell people you are a lady, then you really are not."* If you need to tell people that you are a leader, then you are not a leader. You must carry yourself as a leader. Show people and not disclose them.

The proof of leadership is found in those who follow. The most outstanding leader in the world was Jesus Christ. It does not matter if you think he is the Savior of the World, a Great Prophet, or just a man. You cannot deny his leadership. He was a leader who came from a poor family and born in a stable. Yet, look at his followers. Even today, long after his death, he still has a world of followers. He did not have a title. No, did not hold any position. What he did have was an influence. His influence was felt by the world and is still felt today.

Everyone can be a leader. It does not matter if you are a farmer, homeless, in the military, a cashier, or have a poor family. Look at all the great leaders of the world. How did they lead? Where did they come from? All these great leaders have a few things in common. It is a combination of various traits that will mold an exceptional leader.

Character: This is who you are as a person. The type of surface you are can get you far in your leadership. How are you developing yourself on the inside?

Relationship: These are the people you know. As a leader, you have people who follow you. You must build a relationship with those people to see success in your team. Your relationship with your team says a lot about the type of leader you are. What are you doing to build relationships with your team?

Think about your relationship with those in your group. What can you do to create or strengthen those relationships? Do you know what their families are like or what their interests are? These are fundamental questions to get you to start on finding out who works with you. It may not seem like much; however, it could mean everything to those in your team.

Knowledge: Of course, you already know this. Granted, it will not make you a leader by itself. However, you do not have some ability to be put into a leadership position. I would like to take it one step further and add education. The best way to have experience is through education. This does not mean you should pretend to know everything. You will learn from your team as much as they will learn from you. What are you doing to expand your knowledge?

As a leader, you are always training your team. The significant part about this is how you must prepare for that training. As you qualify, you receive a refresher of what you are teaching and maybe learn something new to share. You will always strive to learn new things. I make a goal to learn something new everyday about my job.

Intuition: It is more of the way you feel. You have probably heard the saying *"a woman's intuition."* It is the way they are feeling about something. I have learned that you never mess with the intuition of a woman. As a leader, you will have your intuition. Some would say, follow your gut feeling. They are really saying follow your intuition about the situation. Think about the leaders you admire. Do they have an instinct when they lead others?

The most outstanding leaders have an instinct to lead. This instinct can be learned or a part of you already. Over time as a leader, you may hone your instincts and become a better leader for doing so.

Experience: This is straight forward. How long have you been a leader? What have you done? How does your team look at you? You would want to take challenges head-on. These challenges are what go you experience.

To see success, you need to find ways to gain experience. This can be accomplished through many different avenues. You could try volunteering or taking on extra jobs at work or with the community.

Success in the Past: They say the past will come back to haunt you. This is true if you have negative issues from your past. However, it takes time to get where you want to be. Do not be afraid to take risks. Learn from your past, and do not let it haunt you. Trust in your leadership, and continue to be successful. Look at every experience from your history as a success.

Ability: Think about everything you can do as a leader. What are your skills? This is what you can do and accomplish. Your skills and abilities will be what gives your team success. You must always be developing new skills. As a leader, you never stop learning.

The abilities you have are determined by your ability to learn. In the military, I was always encouraged to get a degree. Therefore, I would do the same for my team. Having a good education is essential, and for you to be promoted in the military, you need to work on your schooling. That is how crucial it is. In most jobs, you can get hired right out of school. Although you must have a bachelor's or higher to go far in any organization or company.

You have been given the tools for success. You know what it takes to be an exceptional leader. Use those tools and dig deep to find the leader you are meant to be. Change is constant. You must keep up with those changes.

Chapter 16: Defining Your Philosophy

It is time to find your philosophy of leadership. Many will say that style and philosophy are the same.However, they are two different things.

You can have several different styles of leadership. The one thing that drives your individual style is your philosophy. A leader's philosophy is established through their beliefs and the values that drive them. Think of it as a set of rules personally designed for the individual. This is the foundation that makes a foul, excellent, or exceptional leader. It becomes the drive and focuses on guiding their team.

Walk into any company or look at the company you work for right now. Do they have a company philosophy? Most organizations expect their employees to know the philosophy. It will give them direction for their job.Companies' philosophy is not for an individual leader. It is created by the leaders of the company or organization. It is their philosophy.

Keep in mind, the companies philosophy is someone else's. Yet, every leader in the company has its own philosophy that guides them as a leader. This is taken from the different styles of leadership.

Why is Having a Philosophy Important?

Every exceptional leader will have their own individual philosophies. It gives the leader guidance. It helps them stay focus and ensure every task is completed to the standard of the leader. Although it has another purpose. It helps everyone on the team know and understand what is expected of them and the bar. It turns, there is less stress among members of the team and the leadership. Thus, providing more productivity.

Konosuke Matsushita is considered the *"God of Management"* in Japan. He is the founder of Panasonic Japan. He once wrote, *"If you are a leader, you must have an ideology of leadership."* He continues to explain, *"If you lack ideology and attempt to decide everything on a case-by-case basis, you will never be capable of strong leadership."*

If You are a Leader, You Must Have an Ideology of Leadership.

Matsushita hit it on the nose. Ideology is a system that is comprised of ideas and ideas. It becomes clear how important having a philosophy really is. It is to easy to lose our way as a leader and let things go to your head. When this happens, you start to sink towards lousy leadership. You must remember who you are as a leader and what kind of leader you want to be.

What Should be Included in Your Philosophy?

This is a question that haunts me, leaders. One of the most significant mistakes leaders makes taking someone else's philosophy and adapting it to themself. The philosophy must be yours and not theirs. Adapting someone else philosophy still makes it theirs. Your beliefs may not be what they believe.

Your philosophy must be yours. It shows your values as a leader. You will want to show confidence and adaptability. Add your ability to develop your team. Your team wants someone they know they can count on. Add your vision as a leader and your vision for your team. Be sure to make it realistic and obtainable.

One of the most important things you want to portray to your team is trust.Ensure the attributes, values, and beliefs in your philosophy are real and shown through your leadership.

Writing your philosophy is a learning curve. It will not always work the way you want it to work. That is ok. You can always modify and adjust until you have it just right. This allows for self-reflection. Through this time of reflection, it makes you a better leader.

What are the Benefits of Having a Leadership Philosophy?

Having a philosophy that is custom to who you are as a leader comes with several benefits. It shows who you are as a leader. It outlines your expectations for your team, so everyone knows what to expect from the leader. It gives the leader focus and guidance. You will find your philosophy will allow you to avoid making last-minute decisions that are case-by-case. It will provide consistency in all your choices as a leader and for your team.

Each philosophy must be different based on the individual and their roles. Issues one leader may have may not be the same issues another leader with a face. In turn, there are no two leaders who are alike. This is why having a philosophy that is designed for the individual leader is so powerful.

The Hard Truth About Leadership

Defining your leadership philosophy can be difficult. The hard truth, it can be more difficult to define yourself as a leader. The fact is that what you are doing when creating your leadership philosophy. You are expressing yourself as a leader for your team and peers to understand you.

If you are new to being a leader, it can be a struggle. You want to motivate and inspire your team and everyone around you. The hardest part about being new is knowing where to begin.

A truth about leadership is it becomes a moving target. Your leadership will be a continuous and dynamic experience of learning. It will fill the rest of the time of your career.

One thing you must remember about the business world is leadership and management are not connected. It is true! We think that upper-management is the leader of the company. We often associate them together. In reality, you can be in management and not be a leader. The same goes for leaders. Not every leader is cut out to be in command.

There can be good managers, but that does not mean they will be good leaders. Managers make decisions for the company, but they do not always need to guide, inspire, and motivate them. That is the role of the leader. The same for leaders can teach, inspire, and motivate employees and their team, but they may not be able to make decisions for the company. Each has its own role. If you have a company with strong leaders who are also strong managers, you are golden. Yet, this can be rare.

Everyone can hold leadership skills. It does not matter what level in the organization you are. All you need to do is try. You will never know what kind of leader you are if you do not try first.

You may think leadership[is easy, and you can do it alone. Another truth, you can never be a good or exceptional leader by going at it by yourself. When I was a leader, I learned that it is not my ability to guide, influence, motivate and inspire that made me a leader. Those around me, such as my team, friends, family, and other leaders, made me a leader. I owned my ability to lead to them.

It is not about what you can do. It is about working together as a team to make it happen. You have created a philosophy that demonstrates you as a leader. You will find that your philosophy is combined with what you have learned from others and your own beliefs and desires.

An effective leader will learn to work with and connect with their team and those around them. It is a neverending process of learning. You are always learning as a leader.

Those who have compassion for their leadership will not become complacent. You must strive to be the best leader you can.

Creating Your Own Leadership Philosophy

Listen to me talk about philosophy can be tedious. I could go on and on; yet, you will still not fully understand. It is your turn to start putting your leadership philosophy together. Granted, you may have already created one. That is ok. It gives you a chance to reflect on what you have done and make it better.

Your Turn: Put down this book or audio after each step to work through it. If you are driving or do not have the time right now, save this spot or take a mental note. As a quick note, if you are around a computer, use Excel or a spreadsheet application while you go through this. If you are not, eventually transfer it to a spreadsheet and make the same columns. As you go through these steps, you will get an idea of how to design your spreadsheet. This will allow you to be more organized and get a better picture when righting your philosophy.

Step One – Self-Reflection: As a United States Military leader, I saw all leadership types with various leadership styles. Knowing the kind of leader I want to be, I created a leadership philosophy that took all the different leaders' best. I tied their best qualities and put them inline with my own attributes and beliefs. I dod not want to be a leader that everyone looked down upon.

Reflecting on your philosophy is an essential step to creating a philosophy that works for you and your leadership style. If you have not made a philosophy, yet you can still do self-reflection. You can reflect on the kind of leader you would like to be. This step is not a one-time thing, and call it good. An exceptional leader will go over these steps in a continuous loop. They are always learning and finding ways to be a better leader.

Stop and think about everyone who has come into your life. What type of person are they? What are their bad qualities? What are their good qualities? What makes them a bad leader? What makes them a good leader?

Get out a piece of paper and divide it in half. On one-half label it, *"Qualities Others Possess."* On the other half label it, *"Qualities I Possess."* On both halves, you will make two columns. Each half will have a column labeled *"Bad"* and *"good."* Therefore, you will have four columns. It will look similar to this:

Qualities Others Possess		Qualities I Possess	
Bad	Good	Bad	Good

Start with the *"Qualities Others Possess."* Start listing all the qualities you see in others. These qualities can be from leaders, friends, family, and co-workers. Really, anyone who you are associated with. Make note if they are bad qualities or good qualities. Do not move on until you have thought of all the qualities in others. However, you can add to this list at anytime if you think of more. You will also add to this list every time you do a self-reflection of your leadership. Unless things never change in this continuously changing world, there will always be something new to add and reflect on.

Next, do the same for the qualities you possess. Keep in mind, we are only focusing on your rates for this step. Do not worry about what your beliefis. However, your thoughts will play a part with you, even knowing it as you make your list. That is because they are a part of you and are always guiding your actions. With that in mind, you will find it hard to find the bad. Dig deep and find the qualities you do not like. Try to find something. These are usually your weaknesses. Make your list. If you need help, ask those who are closest to you. They can point out areas that you may not see.

Put down these books or audio. If you are driving or do not have the time right now, save this spot or take a mental note. As a quick note, if you are around a computer, use Excel or a spreadsheet application while you go through this. If you are not, eventually transfer it to a spreadsheet and make the same columns. As you go through these steps, you will get an idea of how to design your spreadsheet. This will allow you to be more organized and get a better picture when righting your philosophy.

Step Two – Your Beliefs: The next step is to findout what your beliefs are. You have talked about your qualities. Now, what are your ideas? Your opinions are what defines who you are. Do not jeopardize what you believe for the sake of leadership. An exception leader sticks to their beliefs and allows them to show through their leadership.

Add another column to your spreadsheet. Label it as *"My Beliefs."* It may look like this:

Qualities Others Possess		Qualities I Possess		My
Bad	Good	Bad	Good	Beliefs

In this column, start listing all your beliefs. Dig deep as this will help you better understand who you are as an individual and a leader. You can add or take away from this list as follow your career as a leader and establish your leadership style.

You now have the basics for your lists. These are the foundations of what makes up your leadership style and philosophy.

Step Three – Identify Your Potential Strengths: This area may be challenging for some and more difficult for others. The idea is to focus on how you can turn the bad into strengths. More so, turning the bad into a positive. Therefore, we are going to make two columns for each bad. You will have one labeled *"Negative"* and the other labeled *"Positive."* It will look like this:

Qualities Others Possess		Qualities I Possess		My
Bad	Good	Bad	Good	Beliefs
Negavive	Positive	Negative	Positive	

In the negative column, you will list all the bad. For every bad, you will have a positive. This is a way for you to start turning all the negative habits and make them strengths.

If you have this in a spreadsheet, label the worksheet as Self-Reflection. Open another worksheet and mark it as Leadership Reflection.

Step Four – Leadership Reflection: I know what you are thinking about. You are wondering why we are doing two reflections. The first reflection is to get you thinking about who you are. So many people do not even know who they are. This time you are going to reflect on the type of leader you want to be.

As you reflect on your leadership abilities, you will ask yourself a series of questions. Each question will have a different list.

The first column will be labeled, *"How am I Currently Leading My Team?"* It is essential to know and understand hat you are doing now and what is working and what is not. It may look like this:

How am I Currently Leading My Team?
Attributes	Working	Not Working

This step aims to list all the things you are doing working and find out what is not working and be changed. For you to fully understand your leadership, you need to analyze what you are doing.

The next column will be labeled, *"How Do I Want Others to See Me as a Leader?"* These questions will allow you to reflect on what you want others to think about you. It may uncover new areas that you did not know about in the Self-Reflection, or several of your beliefs will shine through. It may look like this:

How Do I Want Others to See Me as a Leader?

The next column will be labeled *"Differences."* This is for finding any gaps between what you want to do and what you are doing. You will also want to list why they are gaps. It is a chance for you to understand where changes need to be made in what you are doing as a leader. It may look like this:

Differences

Gaps   Why?

I want you to think about the leaders you admire and those you do not like. We can learn alot from other leaders. It does not matter what type of leader they are; there is always something to be discovered. You will make two more questions. One is labeled"Leaders I Admire," and the other is labeled, *"Leaders I Do Not Admire."* It may look like this:

Leaders I Admire   Leaders I Do Not Admire

Leader   Attributes   Leader   Attributes

Remember, it is essential to list the qualities that you like or dislike about those leaders.

Step Five – Bringing It Together: I want you to create one more worksheet in your spreadsheet. This time label it, *"Leadership Philosophy and Principles."* This worksheet will be for you to list all the qualities that align with your two reflections. You can organize it however you would like. My recommendation is this:

Personal   Leadership   How do They Align?

Look at your personal reflection. Analyze your beliefs, the good from others and yourself, and the positive of the bad. List the qualities that fit into your ideas from all the columns and put them in the *"personal"* column. Analyze your answers to the leadership reflection and list them in the *"Leadership"* column.

Now it is time to look at both columns. In the third column, you will determine and list how your leadership attributes are aligned with your personal abilities.

This section will be precious when writing your leadership philosophy. While writing, you may want to continue looking at the entire workbook as a whole.

Step Six – Time to Write and Create: Open up a word document and start brainstorming what you want others to know about your philosophy. Think about everything you may face. You will want to begin with a Leadership Statement. This is like the main idea of your philosophy. It will reflect who you are. Start by asking yourself, *"How do I want my team to see me as a leader?"* Think about your personal beliefs and leadership goals. This is where everything starts to come together.

Next, you may want to list your standards and expectations. Again, these expectations will be inline with your leadership and personal beliefs. You will want to make it very clear what you expect. You have high standards; make sure your teams know this through your philosophy.

Along with your expectations, your team will have expectations of you as their leader. Therefore, you will want to mention what you will do for them. It is like making a promise. They promise to uphold your expectations, and you promise to be an exceptional leader.

Following these steps will point you in the right direction to become an exceptional leader with an excellent philosophy. Be the leader your team wants you to be. Your example will mold future leaders.

Chapter 17: Abusive Leadership and Avoiding Becoming Abusive

You have probably been in a situation with an abusive leader. These are traits that are not tolerated in any workplace. This type of leadership does not span to only the team.

Even leaders find themselves dealing with an abusive leader. How do you deal with these types of situations? As a leader, how do you avoid becoming an abusive leader yourself? What can a manager do to protect their leaders and employees from having this type of situation in their organization? These are issues and questions managers face every day. So, what do you do?

Coping with Abusive Leaders

Employees under the supervision of an abusive leader should determine how to cope with them or get out of that situation. They need to look for ways to find a better way to relieve themselves of theposition and find better people to guide them. A better way to view this came from the words of Abraham Lincoln when he said, *"Be with a leader when they are right, stay with them when theyare still right, but leave them when they are wrong."*

Be with a Leader when They are Right. Stay with Them when They are Still Right, but Leave Them when They are Wrong.

Bad bosses can show up in every industry. The behaviors associated with being an abusive leader are integrated from personal emotions.For employees to disassociate from these types of people, they need to develop skills to recognize one first then create a strategy on how to manage them. Here issome example!

Consider looking for another job with a better environment: A different workplace is better than having a toxic boss. It is better to head to another company than enduring a demanding boss just to keepyour job. A positive working environment should always be the main priority for an employee to look for a job.

It is essential to have an open and welcoming workplace rather than feeling hostility. Look for a company that says otherwise, get feedback from other people, especially the tenure who have been with the company for a while and be practical to relay your previous experience to the management; chances are you will be likely to work with an impressive leader.

Team up with people with the same concerns: Employees who work together with the same circumstances are stronger together. Especially if they are concerns about having a demanding boss and a hostile environment. If the system is at fault, employees can work together to relay the upper management's concern, creating a solution.

Never underestimate the power of people working together. If they have the same concern or vision, they can figure it out and work through the difficult times.

Keep your distance: Remember the saying, "*Ignorance is bliss,*" as it is a compelling method to avoid difficult bosses. Simply ignoring them and not making yourself involve will make you more productive at work. Manage simple ways to prevent them, such as not bringing yourself to gatherings outside of work, reporting to him only if necessary, and working as much as possible online. Make yourself familiar with the rules, too; this will get you to a safer place.

Remain optimistic: Remind yourself that every unfortunate situation shall pass.Focus on your work and direct your attention to what is more important. Strive harder and understand the reason for these moments, which probably is making you healthier or meant to teach you something. After all, if you do not change, you will never learn.

Being optimistic can be very difficult. It takes work and practice. Take it as a challenge and strive to be confident at all times.

Do not fan the flames: If your boss is picking on you, avoid being aggressive.Difficult bosses often prey on the weakest individual, and those who fight back are the ones who were bullied more. It is better to put out flames before it could get any worse. Do not openly talk about your boss behind your back, stay professional and mature, and leave the upper management reprimand.Do not do anything to undermine the situation; if you do, chances are, they will take this back on you personally.

Take It to the Manager

I wanted to bring these things into this chapter to understand what their employees are doing. You will find abusive leadership in every aspect of an organization. No matter how much you try, it cannot be prevented entirely.

If the organization is significant, the management cannot see everything that goes on. That is why it is essential to have an open-door policy for all your employees or a way to report a leader without them knowing.

An abusive leader will punish those who report them. That is why it is essential to have these different routes to inform management. The hardest part you will face is what to do once you discover this type of leader within your organizat on. Ultimately, the decision is that of the manager. Here are a few ideas, but you do not need to limit yourself to only these.

- ➢ Leadership Training
- ➢ Probation
- ➢ Demotion
- ➢ Suspension
- ➢ Termination

Some of these may seem extreme. However, it may be necessary if you have run out of other options. You may even consider the next section on Servant Leadership to help them learn to be better leaders.

Servant Leadership

A great founder and author, Robert K. Green, once said, *"The servant-leader is a servant first. It begins with the natural feeling that one wants to serve, to serve first."* The author believes that servant leadership is the true essence of leadership. The act of leading must be to create change inindividuals' lives, build better organization, influence and motivate people to choose the right path, and, most of all, create a better world.

The Servant-Leader is a Servant First. It Begins with the Natural Feeling that One wants to Serve.

Servant leaders aim to continue developing their team, making them the future leaders as well.

Volunteering: Through volunteerism, a person develops character such as being selfless, generous, and becoming aware of their surroundings. In recent times, volunteers play a vital role in making our world a better place to live. They bring countless differences in the lives of many people, and it benefits both ways too! Volunteers get to help those people in need while receiving lessons of awareness in return. Once a volunteer is aware of theirsurroundings, they will commit to changing it, making it better.

Servant leaders are non-judgmental: They focus on delivering results rather than giving too much attention to their insecurities and non-essential things.Putting labels on items only destroys trust and connections, which binds a team together.

Leaders are willing to sacrifice: Servant leaders are willing to sacrifice to add value to what they do. They acknowledge that leadership will always be connected to risk and sacrifice. They understand that tosee success, they must experience failure. They may be sacrificing time with their family or financial sacrifice but are willing to do it in exchange to create a difference.

Develop other leaders: One of the primaryresponsibilities of a leader is to create more leaders. They believe that if more humane and just leaders will rule an immediate society or organization, this world will become better.

Leadership is a legacy. They receive the challenge of becoming a leader in passing it on to others. One big difference a leader can make is to develop and create more great leaders.

Share your mistakes with others: Mistakes should be taken as a lesson that is not treated as a waste opportunity. If a leader had done something wrong, then they should take it as a chance to become better of himself.

Personal experience is a great teacher, and a missed opportunity is a lesson learned. Servant leaders value their own experiences; may it be bad or good.

Build trust and give trust: Trust is a hard-earned trait. Servant leaders recognize the importance of building trust in people to gain their confidence. By doing so, loyalty is cultured, and performance is done better.

Servant leaders create a network of support for their team members to create a pleasant working environment. It is essential for employees to feel safe to share their ideas and be trusted. This will give them more confidence to stay in the company and perform at their best.

Open-minded: Great leaders are open-minded people. They accept the reality of having weaknesses and limitations. They know for a fact that they still have a lot to learn. They are open to any opportunities and ideas shared by their people. Admitting their weakness opens to other essential qualities such as vulnerability, honesty, and integrity, vital in leadership.

Exceptional Leaders are the Experts

Being an exceptional leader is an expert in helping their team through demanding situations. They would be the leader your team feels comfortable about approaching when they see anabusive leader. An exceptional leader will also see the concerns and be the first to bring it to the management's attention.

Exceptional leadership is rare. I spent several years of evaluation of my leaders and their leadership styles. I seldom came across someone who I would consider an outstanding leader. I saw many good and bad leaders. I had leaders who I would follow into combat. However, I saw some who I would not follow into a store to by bread.

Exceptional leaders are good leaders who go the extra mile to be memorable. They are the ones who are admired by their team.

They have great people skills: Leadership is all about people.An interpersonal relationship is the foundation of good leadership. A connection to people is vital for a successful leadership journey. It is within the people the success of a leader is based on.

After all, one cannot merely be called a leader without having people to lead. A great leader knows how to create a connection with people, producing results for them and with them. They value the importance of personal relationships with people through listening, being sympathetic, and providing constant help when needed.

They are effective communicators: Informing a connection with people, a leader always starts with words. Mastery of articulation is a success integrator for a leader. So is cultivating acceptable communication practices such as speaking more preciseterms, maintaining positive physical gestures, knowledge of speech, and validating one's words through actions.

Influential leaders serve as an effective leader by hearing their people's voices using dialogue; communication is a two-way process after all. They communicate to their people by knowing their hopes, aspirations, and dreams then turning them into reality.

They encourage other people to grow: A United States President once said,*"The greatest leaders are not necessarily the ones who do the greatest things.They are the ones who get people to do great things."*To be a great leader is to be a significant influencer. They develop methods to make people listen and follow them, directing them to a more concrete path. They serve as an example of the direction they want their team to choosing from. They promote an environment where people can thrive to become better versions of themselves at their own pace.

A more significant leader knows how to unlock the real potential of their people. They create a network of support for their people to pull off in times of discouragement. They encourage them from the first day they started as beginners until they become triumphant.

Chapter 18: Leadership Assessments

Leadership assessments are designed to help management make big decisions about the leaders of the organization. These can be used to decide on placement, selection, and promotion. They are also used for several different reasons. That makes me wonder, *"Can I use the same tools to assess my own leadership?"*

I have introduced you to a lot of information. At this point, you may want to stop reading for a bit and think about all the information you have been given. Compare them to yourself. Several tools could be used to help you with your assessment. Some of these you may have heard of while others you may not have.

DiSC

Some leaders say this is one of the most used and most popular tools for assessing your leadership. I personally have not used this tool. However, some leaders think it is very accurate and useful. It is straightforward to use.

The DISC system will measure behavior through observation. However, other systems focus more on the preferences of the individual. You can also use a more advanced version of DiSC that will compare work and home. The nice thing about DiSC is the wide variety of tests and will have different types of quality based on your needs. The best thing to do is to choose a test with top reviews and an organization you trust.

Each letter of DiSC stands for the four primary styles of the assessment.

- ➢ D = Dominance
- ➢ i = Influence
- ➢ S = Steadiness
- ➢ C = Conscientiousness

Knowing the primary styles will help you better understand the 12 different combinations your leadership may fall into. I will first introduce the four primary types. Then I will break down the eight other varieties that are possible.

D – action, results, and challenge: This style aims to achieve bottom-line results and personal victory. You fear you looking weak infront of your team and do not want to be taken advantage of. You are insistent, competitive, and assertive. You must win. It is always a competition, and the situation is still a win/lose. Your effectiveness will be increased through patience and empathy.

i – action, enthusiasm, and collaboration: You always feelthe excitement. You want to feel the popularity, and you seek approval for what you are doing. You fear being rejected and not receiving an acknowledgment. You are influenced by the contagious energy of others, their personal charm, and their optimism.Your optimism, enthusiasm, and the need for praise can be overbearing. You will increase your effectiveness through the completion of your tasks and your objectivity.

S – stability, support, and collaboration: Your goal is to create harmony within your team and give them strength. You fear the rapid changes that come unexpectedly. You also fear letting down your team and others who are counting on you. You are easily influenced by the friendliness and collaboration of your team. You will use your modesty, compromises, and passive resistance more than is needed. Your effectiveness as a leader will increase by showing your self-confidence and your real feelings.

C – stability, accuracy, and challenge: You are all about the figures and results. Your goal is based on accuracy and analysis. You like the objective processes that are tried and true. You have a fear of being wrong. You do not enjoy how your emotions show through—you are influenced by the standards. Everything must be done correctly, logically, and to the bar. You will achieve analysis paralysis and personal restraint abundantly. You can increase your effectiveness by looking past all the data, listening to your team, and acknowledging how they feel.

DC – results, challenge, and accuracy: You have a goal for independence and accomplishments. You fear that you will not achieve the standards you set for you and your team. You are influenced by having high standards that have been developed and a determination to meet those standards. You have a tendency to be too blunt or sarcastic. You may have a condescending attitude. Your effectiveness will increase through personal warmth and having tactful communications.

Di – results, action, and enthusiasm: You take advantage of new opportunities through your quick thinking or actions. You fear losing your personal power that you worked so hard to achieve. You will be influenced by the bold stories or charming personalities of your team. You overdo it with your manipulation, egoism, and impatience. You will indeed show an increase in your effectiveness by learning patience and humility. It is also essential to learn to be more considerate of your team and those you work with.

iD – enthusiasm, action, and results: You are always on the lookout for the next breakthrough and exciting opportunity. You do not like having a fixed environment, and you fear losing the attention you are using. You always want to do your best so that you do not lose the approval of your leader. The creative thinking of others will easily influence your decisions. You tend to be too impulsive and outspoken. You will do well as a leader to learn to focus more and listen better to the details. This will increase your effectiveness.

iS – enthusiasm, collaboration, and support: You seek friendship and enjoy cooperation with your team. You fear being disliked by your team and do not want to bring extra pressure. The empathy of others will affect and influence your decision making. You may have too much patience and tend to approach issues indirectly. You could increase your leadership effectiveness by learning to confront the problems and be objective about your team.

Si – support, collaboration, and enthusiasm: Being accepted and having close relationships with your team is essential to you. You fear confrontation. You do not like being pressured by your team. You are influenced by the patience and empathy of your team. You have not found the balance with your work, kindness, and personal connections as you show to much of the latter two. The best thing you can do is learn to say *"no"* when needed and confront the issues.

SC – support, stability, accuracy: You enjoy a calm environment. It is essential that there is a steady pace towards your goal or to finish the task. You fear chaos. You do not like the unknown. You hate deadlines as they provide too much pressure to meet a task's needs in the required time. You are influenced by consistency and self-control. You are the leader, yet you are willing to let others take the lead as you shy back into your office. It would be good to add to your effectiveness by taking the initiative on tasks and speaking up when needed.

CS – accuracy, stability, and support: You want peace and a reliable outcome. You get emotional over the change in situations. You are influenced by the practice approach. It is essential to pay attention to details. You are to traditional and take caution. You are not a risk-taker. You do not like trying new things. You need to stick with the methods that work and have been tested. You will become an exceptional leader if you learn to be more flexible in how you do things and show a sense of urgency.

CD – accuracy, challenge, and results: You know that efficient products will come from your rational decisions. You fear of personal failure and your lack of control. Strick standards are one of your biggest influencers. You have a sort of bluntness and a critical attitude towards your team. It would be an excellent benefit for you to learn to pay more attention to your team and learn cooperation.

There is so much to be learned through the DISC assessment. Which combination do you think you fall into?

Myers-Briggs Type Indicator (MBTI)

One of the most known is the Myers-Briggs Type Indicator. In fact, the military uses this for there leaders. It was first introduced to the world in 1962. Its primary purpose is for teams. It divides each leader into 16 different types of personalities. These combinations will be based on four other letters.

- ➢ E = Extraversion or I = Interoversion
- ➢ S = Sensing or N = Intuition
- ➢ T = Thinking or F = Feeling
- ➢ J = Judging or P = Perceiving

This assessment gives a great understanding of who you are as a leader. It is extensive but accurate. When you take the official test, it will provide you with the four-letter code and its name, but it will also give you an in-depth explanation of what it means.

Gallup Strengthsfinder

This assessment tool is among the best to use for your leaders. It focuses more on strengths and not the weaknesses, behaviors, or preferences. The great thing about this is it helps a leader become positive. When the leader has more positivity, the team is more productive and motivated. Talking about your team's weaknesses could bring down moral. However, as this assessment focuses on the strengths, the ethical will stay high.

There is a list of around 30 possible strengths. The assessment will narrow it down to your top 5 strengths. It is a great tool to build up your team with.

Saville Assessment

This assessment has a massive variety of different skills that will be covered. They include skills in numerical, error checking, spatial, mechanical, and verbal. Overall, the assessment can be divided into two different categories. You will have your aptitude test and your personality tests.

I want to focus on personality questionnaires. These will look at your personality in the workplace and your behavioral preferences. There are two different questionnaires. You will have a short version and an extended version. Depending on how much detail you need will determine the type you use. The extended version will take you about 40 minutes from start to finish. However, within those 40 minutes, you are assessing recommended culture-orientation fit, strengths, and weaknesses. You will also identify your behavior and ability fits through a number series. This assessment can be used on your team to help you find the best way to lead them and be the most effective.

These are only a few of the top assessment tools for leadership and your team. However, there are several free assessments available and are based on the same strategies as these. Keep in mind, you get what you paid for. That means they are not s good as these that I have listed here.

Use these tools to assess your leadership. However, use them to evaluate your team as well. These are great tools to help develop your team and find the areas they could work on or strengthen to become a fantastic leader.

Chapter 19: Knowledge and Inspiration for the Exceptional

Every leader tends to burnout and gets frustrated. There is no way around that. The big question is, what do you do about it?How can you avoid it? Exceptional leaders have this down. They know how to control the burnout and balance home and work and still functionas they are supposed to.

Now that you have assessed your philosophy and leadership style, it is time for knowledge and more wisdom. There are a few things that will help you cope. Read through each of these and internalize and compare it to your own leadership. How do they relate?How do they help you?

Our Team is Why You an Exceptional Leader

The best leaders are not always smart people on the team. No, really! You do not need to know everything. In fact, the stronger your crew, the healthier you are as a leader. Remember, you are only an exceptional leader because you have an outstanding team.

As a leader, you will want to pick up the slack. If you do not have a strong team, make them healthy. Use the tips and tricks throughout this book and create a strong team. Train them and teach them how to be healthy. Focus on areas that need to be improved in the training and use their strengths to bring up the team's rest to the same level.

We are Human and Make Mistakes, Too

There is no perfect leader. The best leaders even make mistakes. When they make a mistake, they own it. They will not blame others,such as their team. They know why the mistake was made. They except this and move on. An exceptional leader will learn from the mistake and ensure it is not made again.

Knowledge is a powerful tool. I always say, *"Knowledge is Power."* As you learn from your mistakes, you gain the experience to succeed next time.

Knowledge is Power.

Give Away Your Power and Receive 10-Fold

Think about it, you have the power to give others strength. You can allow your team members to take charge of a meeting with your training. You provide them with the ability to lead. You guide them and set them up for success. In return, it makes you a better mentor and guide. A better leader, as you allowed them to strengthen their own leadership abilities. Thus, creating a stronger team.

Personal Healthy is Essential in Leadership

It does not matter how busy you are. You must take care of yourself, mentally, and physically. This will give you the energy to lead and a strong team. If we cannot be healthy, our leadership will not be beneficial. Our team will not be healthy, and productivity will be down.

Your health is a significant part of your leadership ability. Every morning I go walking to stay physically fit. My spouse makes a fantastic breakfast full of nutrients that give me energy. I spend a few minutes to myself to help me get focused. Sometimes this is done through meditation. Other times it is coloring on my tablet. Find a way for you to get healthy. Energy through food and exercise is essential. However, what do you do to stay mentally fit?

It is Not Your Job to *"Fix"* People

You are not a people fixer. In fact, you cannot fix others. The more you try, the more you will fail. You need to set the example and instill goodness into your team. The only people fixer is themselves.

Do not focus on what you cannot change. Focus on what you can do to help your team develop within themselves.

Too Much Communication Does Not Exist

Have you ever played the telephone game? Communication within your team is like the telephone game. The more time that passes, the more information is lost. You want to continuously communicate and update your unit. Most leaders share early in the project what is needed to succeed. However, if this communication stops, the team will fail and not know what is expected. Over time, they will forget what the expectations are. That is why it is essential to keep the line of communication alive within the team.

Do not play the telephone game with work. That is like risking the entire project. Be the one who passes down the information, and you do not let your team jump to conclusions or speculations.

You Have the Power to Affect the Lives of Others

The power is yours. You cannot fix people; however, you can change their lives based on your actions. Sometimes, this can be through an email, phone call, meeting, company party, or a bonus for a special occasion such s Christmas.

Leaders may not always remember the things they do to impact the lives of others. That is ok. It does not make them a bad leader. Although, they do reflect the impact that their contributions and actions have on others and the team.

Your Team Have Separate Lives Outside the Office

It is essential to remember your team members have lives outside of the office. They came from different experiences, interests, backgrounds, family cultures, problems, and personalities. Expecting them to not be at work when scheduled is not realistic and is unproductive. Understand the lives of your team and take them into consideration.

This is a great way to get to know who is on your team. Find out about their families and what they like when not at work. What are their interests? Get to know their families and create a relationship with your team members and their families. Remember special days. If it is essential to your team member, it is necessary for you. Be excited to hear about their interests. After all, they are eager to tell you about it.

As a leader, I always went out of my way to find out about my employees. If they tell me about something they are doing, I remember to ask them about it. For example, if they go to Yellowstone National Park with their family, I will ask them how the trip was when they get back. Even if it was during the weekend, and they did not miss any days for the journey. The same goes for if their daughter has a dance recital. I will remember she had a recital and will ask about it. If you have a strong relationship with your team, they will be excited to share pictures or a video of it.

The Rules Can Be Broken at Times

The policies and rules of an organization or for your team are not set in stone. Sometimes, you must bend a little if it affects theproductivity and effectiveness of the group. They are only used as a guide. Know when it is okay to break the rules and when it is not. This is your team, you are the leader, and you must make the decision of less resistance.

Most of the time, rules that seem like they are commonsense are only there because it was needed. Do not think of it as breaking the rules. Think of it as being creative to get the job done most effectively. If you see a direction that does not make sense, question it with upper management and give your reasons.

Your Team Members are Always Changing

People will transfer in and out of your team. Maybe they are moved to another department or unit. Perhaps they are promoted and put into a leadership position themselves. They could even make a change in their career. Whatever the reason, that is ok. You are a great leader. You most likely had a hand in their development so they can make this critical decision. They will remember the outstanding leadership you gave and your fantastic example. They will take the thing you have taught and will apply it to their next chapter in life.

Be humble and grateful that you had them on your team. This will free up space to introduce a new member to the team and help mold them as the leaders you know they can be. Perhaps, there may be a time you meet your old team members and see the great things they are doing. You never know, they may be your boss one day.

Do not fear change. Embrace change and use it as a growing experience. You can also use this experience for an opportunity for growth within your team. It happens all the time in the military. Leaders are always getting new soldiers on their teams. They must adapt to each one and guide them the same as the rest of the group.

We Can Not Do Everything Well

You are not perfect. You make mistakes, perform your job, and lead a team. Yet, there is still room for improvement. An exceptional leader knows what they need to do and where to best spend their time. Do not try to be a straight-A student at work. It is impossible. Set expectations that are obtainable and reasonable.

Focus on what you can do and not what you cannot do. Time is money! Remember, time management. Use your time wisely and achieve what you can, knowing you are giving it your all and doing your best.

When I was young, I had a job work at a movie theatre. I worked at the box office, and the concessions stand. It was my job to take the money and ensure moviegoers were satisfied. I was not a leader, yet I showed leadership. My boss took the time to train me in the different areas of the job. Eventually, I was in charge when the boss or supervisor could not be there. I was not officially in leadership positions, but I was a leader.

Inspiration Through the Numbers

For me, I do not pay much attention to the numbers. However, for managers, CEOs, and some other leaders, it is all about the numbers. They can provide inspiration to motivate your team to do better. I have handpicked facts that are dealing with leadership. Through these numbers, you will see why it is essential to have exceptional leadership within the organization.

In 2020, around 79% of employees quit their job or leave their position based on the leadership's lack of appreciation. That is a lot of people who do not have the direction they deserve. There are great leaders; however, there are leaders who are not as great. They are the ones who have been causing an increase in unemployment and job changes.

The lack of leadership development is a significant concern. We must develop our new leaders in the future. About 69% of Millennials believe there is a lack in this area. That gives you an idea of one place that needs immediate attention. As a back up to leadership development, only about 5% of the companiesintegrate leadership development within their organization. It is no wonder why 69% of Millennials see this area is lacking.

We are training the future leaders of the world. Sadly, out of the leaders, many of them lackthe knowledge to train future leaders. Only about 14% of CEOS have a talent for leading and guide the organization. If the leaders in higher positions lack there are no wonders, there is no development program.

Most of the leaders in higher positions are not used to the digital world. They do not like change and cannot adapt. Around 16% of organizations will have success in the digital marketing world. That is because the older generations of leaders do not conform to the time. They are set in their ways and are ready to retire.

As a leader, it is essential to confirm the times and accept change.Future leaders will be made up of Millennials. In fact, about 75% will be our leaders by 2025. This is the same generation that says organizations are lacking in leadership development. How can we expect them to buy the future if we cannot even get the leadership development under control? Where will the business, organizations, and non-profits be if we do not develop them as leaders?

Ever wondered why some candidates turn down a good job? The answer is simple. 9.15% turn down the offer once they see there is a negative working culture in the organization. The workplace is like a home away from home. They want to work in a place that they feel comfortable and see the best chance for advancement. In fact, about &0% of employees are not happy at work for this exact reason. They do not enjoy the gloomy atmosphere.

On a better note, 78% of business leaders are focused on their engagements with their teams. They seek ways to improve employee relations.

The older generations are expected to work hard. For example, Baby Boomers know how to work hard. They know if they do not work hard, they do not eat or cannot take care of their families. Therefore, the Millennials will start to feel burnout in a job faster. Many of them had things handed to them, such as technology. If there is not a mobile phone or a high-tech computer, they are lost. Today, it is all about the gadgets.

Due to a poor leadership development program within organizations, about 38% of the new leaders will see failure within 18 months of their leadership. Failure is ok if you learn from it. I believe you must know toknowthe inability to understand how to succeed.

An exceptional leader will set the example. Unfortunately, about 10% of CEOs set an example for the leaders in the organization. That 10% of CEOS are the natural leader and knows the impact of setting an example.

Being an engaged leader is very important in guiding a successful team. Your job is to inspire your team and recommend them to be great leaders. However, only 2.6% of the management or highly engaged as a leader. That is a deficient number. Based on the number alone, they lack the skills and training to work on the other issues and help bring the national statistics.

I could go on and on with the numbers. You can see how leadership needs work throughout the nation and possibly the world. Some areas need to be significantly improved. Remember, it is your job to educate future generations. Mold them into the leaders they are meant to be. They deserve a fantastic leader and not a statistical one. Be the leader they want you to be and guide them to be the organization's future and the world.

Chapter 20: Conclusion

Leadership is all around us. You have seen leadership on the street, in the home, in the office, and wherever you may least expect it. You can find it in all shapes and forms. There are bad leaders, good leaders, and exceptional leaders. The goal is to be an outstanding leader.

Being exceptional is not easy. It takes work and dedication. Your eyes have been opened to different types of leadership. It is up to you which type you focus on. No one can lead you to the right path of leadership except for you.

When you first become a leader, put into a leadership role, it may be a struggle. You may feel lost and unsure. You may question your decisions and the choices you make. The truth is, we have all been there. Even the most influential leaders in history had their struggles. Yet they become exceptional leaders who fought for what they believed in.

Do not think that it ends after reading this book. Take control and be the leader you always wanted to be. Learn from the leaders of the past and be a leader of the future. Do not become a bad leader. You are better than that. Show the world what you can do. Be influential. Martin Luther King Jr. fought for what he believed in with his *"I Have a Dream…"* speech. He did not know it then, but history has shown how influential he was in thepast.

You have the potential to be an exceptional leader. Learn the techniques and strategies I have talked about. Read through the different leadership styles. Think about the kind of leader you would like to be. Plan how you will achieve that high standard of leadership and create your own personal leadership philosophy. Stay clear of abusive leadership styles but learn to handle them when the issue arises.

Successful leadership stories do not happen overnight. Most prominent leaders did not become famous and sought out with only a few bumps in the road. There are no exceptional leaders who would perceive leadership as easy and a walk in the park. Most of them had their own fair share of stories to tell, yet it is with challenges and failure a person builds their character.

What is constant in leading is the challenge it brings, may it be the people they are leading or the circumstances they are facing. Leadership always has its own trade-offs. It comes in many forms, such as internally identified as identity shift and any non-work-related issues, or externally such as the world's globalization and modernization. Not all require the same leadership style, which adds to the difficulty of the challenge.

An effective and efficient leader acknowledges the vital role of change in the delivery of positive results. Yet they know how to manage their resources and mobilize their abilities to manage the unwanted effects of change. A leader adopts the constraint demands of change by changing its leadership style based on their team's personality, which is more applicable to a workplace and depending on the circumstances. They deliver their vision into reality, despite the higher demand for the world's changing pace.

All leaders have their own varying experiences and approaches to the definition of leadership. They also have their own perceptions of different methods and qualities necessary for effective leadership; hence, leadership's true meaning lies in a leader's personal experience. Many experts, for instance, those writers of countless books, famous leaders of their own country, or a small community church leader, would agree on certain principles to effective leadership, yet ultimately acknowledge the most critical factor of leading is producing results.

An effective leader is somebody who brings a specific change in the lives of many people. What makes a leader great are the successful leadership stories they tell. They become efficient by making a significant impact on the businesses they serve. For example, ahead of the family is called a great father if he produces competent graduated children, or a country president is to be considered successful if he sets the economy up. Leadership is always about the differences they make either to a situation or to the lives of many. As John Quincy Adams said, *"If your actions inspire others to dream more, learn more, do more and become more; you are a leader."* They are the catalyst of change, and great leaders are known to be influencers and motivators.

If Your Actions Inspire Others to Dream More, Learn More, Do More, and Become More, You are a Leader.

The most significant achievement of being a leader is by producing more leaders. The true essence of being a leader is not with the number of people who follow them but rather the amount of another leader they make. A leader must be the most excellent motivator in encouraging people to follow their lead. They lead by example, setting themselves the best representation of how a leader must be. They motivate people through words, actions, and practice servant leadership to highlight the importance of serving people.

A famous saying about leadership says, *"Leaders are not born, but made"* because they are. Reaching alone a higher position itself is already indispensable difficult, let alone keeping the part for as long as it takes. It requires many years of practice and continuous learning and development to become effective in leading.

A typical title of a leader alone cannot justify the essential meaning of leadership. Leadership is a process, and learning comes in both ways; they learn from the people they lead orknow something from the leader. It is about both sacrificing and risking too many factors to become fortunate. Thus, embarking on a journey of leadership is changing all the aspects of a person's life.

I live you with the quote from Ralph Waldo Emerson that says, *"Do not follow where the path may lead. Go instead, where there is no path and leave a trail."*

Do Not Follow Where the Path May Lead. Go Instead where there is No Path and Leave a Trail.

Take the assessment and use it to evaluate your own leadership. This helps determine if anything needs to change in what you are doing and see a clearer picture of your leadership. Become the leader you are destined to be. Be great!Be amazing! Be exceptional!

Finally, if you enjoyed this book, please let me know your thoughts with a short review on Amazon. All that you need to do is to click the blue link next to the yellow stars that says "customer reviews." You'll then see a gray button that says "Write a customer review"—click that and you're good to go. It means a lot, thank you!

Brent

.